Social Semiotics Interpretation of Televised Advertising

电视广告的
社会符号学解读

王京京 著

北京师范大学出版集团
BEIJING NORMAL UNIVERSITY PUBLISHING GROUP
安徽大学出版社

图书在版编目(CIP)数据

电视广告的社会符号学解读:英文/王京京著. —合肥:安徽大学出版社,2022.10
ISBN 978-7-5664-2475-4

Ⅰ.①电… Ⅱ.①王… Ⅲ.①影视广告－符号学－研究－英文 Ⅳ.①F713.851

中国版本图书馆 CIP 数据核字(2022)第 160826 号

电视广告的社会符号学解读
Dianshi Guanggao De Shehui Fuhaoxue Jiedu

王京京 著

出版发行	北京师范大学出版集团 安 徽 大 学 出 版 社 (安徽省合肥市肥西路 3 号 邮编 230039) www.bnupg.com www.ahupress.com.cn
印　　刷	安徽利民印务有限公司
经　　销	全国新华书店
开　　本	710 mm×1010 mm　1/16
印　　张	15
字　　数	375 千字
版　　次	2022 年 10 月第 1 版
印　　次	2022 年 10 月第 1 次印刷
定　　价	49.00 元

ISBN 978-7-5664-2475-4

策划编辑:李　雪　　　　　　　　　装帧设计:李　军
责任编辑:李　雪　　　　　　　　　美术编辑:李　军
责任校对:葛灵知　　　　　　　　　责任印制:赵明炎

版权所有　侵权必究
反盗版、侵权举报电话:0551—65106311
外埠邮购电话:0551—65107716
本书如有印装质量问题,请与印制管理部联系调换。
印制管理部电话:0551—65106311

本书是皖西学院2019安徽高校人文社会科学研究项目(SK2019A0434)最终科研成果。在书稿撰写过程中,皖西学院曾必好教授给予作者全程的指导和帮助,并参与了全书的策划、书稿的修改和内容的最终审定工作。

Preface

When a western political system poses the problems of how to communicate and persuade the potential voters to accept their leadership to the politicians, the application of political publicity has become one of the best choices in terms of its convenience and efficiency in the realization of their political objectives. The present study focused on the analysis of campaign advertising in the US general election of the latest three election cycles from the year of 2008 to 2016 as a case study from the semiotic perspective of Multimodal Critical Discourse Analysis (MCDA). It centered on its deliberate design of meaning-making in language along with the artistic creations like image composition, coloring and presentation of identities from the angles of comprehensive and comparative study on both verbal and visual modes. Based on the analysis of the distribution of the multimodality in televised political advertising, it also analyzed the cooperation among those co-existing modes, revealing the buried ideas of power and ideology in multimodal political discourse.

Adopting qualitative research method, the study was underpinned on Benoit's functional approach to political discourses, Halliday's Systemic-Functional Grammar (SFG) and Kress and Van Leeuwen's Visual Grammar (VG). Two hundred minutes' campaign advertisements were collected, sorted and further divided into categories on the basis of the two functions: positive televised advertising and negative ones. Then, the variables of the three meta-functions in SFG were primarily defined for the analysis of the verbal modes, while the variables in VG were defined for the analysis of the visual modes. After that, the comprehensive study on the cooperation of two modes as a coherent whole was conducted. Quantitatively, Antconc for lexicon was utilized.

Thorough analysis of distribution of various variables in verbal and visual modes revealed that meaning construction in political campaign adverting was apparently context-based and function-oriented for better control of thought and much proper manipulation of power. With the main purpose of delivering expected information, similarities in both positive and negative advertising were identified. Material processes in terms of ideational function were most frequently employed to enhance its force of objectivity and persuasion. As for interpersonal function, various mood systems were distributed. Among interpersonal function, declarative clauses in verbal modes and "offer image" in visual modes with the same effect as material processes were the most preferable. However, for the construction of opposite identities and social relations in either positive or negative advertising, the distribution of modal auxiliaries and personal pronouns were different. Corresponding visual elements like size of frame, distance, perspective and modality were employed. Two relations were defined in terms of visual-verbal interactions for better ideological control and power dominance: Ideational elaborations specified and concretized the abstract concepts in verbal modes and in turn, limited the viewers' unbounded imagination; interpersonal extension could supply necessary attitudinal information. All in all, positive advertising aims to balance the factors of certainty, reliability, possibility dominance in power and solidarity in common interest, while negative advertising can mainly show uncertainty, distrust, incompetence and alienation.

The present study made a thorough elaboration on the theoretical evolvement of MCDA. It proved the feasibility and applicability of the MCDA in the process of analyzing the interpersonal meaning of the campaign advertising. In addition, these findings will contribute to the improvement of advertising design and public speaking analysis. It is hoped that this book will continue to serve as a relatively accessible introduction to the field of MCDA. Foreign language learners in China who are always exposed to alien culture and ideology are suggested to read this book so as to cultivate their critical view towards the flood of fake information crowded in the mass media of western countries. The book can be used by graduate students majoring in foreign linguistics and applied linguistics.

My thanks should go to my colleagues in West Anhui University, for their support, encouragement and companion. Special appreciation should go to Professor Zeng Bihao, Dean of School of Foreign Studies in West Anhui University, for his constant encouragement, guidance, inspiration, patience as well as enlightening critiques in mentoring my book. My deepest gratitude should go to my family members: my beloved wife, Xu Jiayun, for her devotion and love to the family; my parents, for their education and support; my son, Wang Xusheng, whose happiness and growth inspire me to pursue a better future.

Due to limited knowledge, time and resources, the present study recommends more data for more precise future researches, criticism and suggestions. Most importantly, I would like to express my deepest gratitude to all those who have helped me through all these years with patience, encouragement and love.

Wang Jingjing
March 2022

Contents

Chapter I
Introduction 1
1.1 Background of the Study 1
1.2 Research Purpose 4
1.3 Significance of the Research 9
1.4 Statement of the Problems 10

Chapter II
Review of Related Literature 11
2.1 Social Semiotic Foundation 11
2.2 Sapir-Whorf Hypothesis 16
2.3 From CDA to MCDA 20
2.4 Modes Contributing to Meaning-making 28

Chapter III
Televised Political Advertising 37
3.1 Political Advertising 37
3.2 American General Election Campaign Advertising 40

Chapter IV
Theoretical Framework ……………………………………… 45
  4.1 Benoit's Functional Approach to Political Discourse …… 45
  4.2 Systemic-functional Grammar ……………………………… 46
  4.3 Visual Grammar ……………………………………………… 55
  4.4 Image-text Relations ………………………………………… 74
  4.5 Research Paradigm of the Study …………………………… 75

Chapter V
Research Methodology …………………………………… 77
  5.1 Research Design ……………………………………………… 77
  5.2 Corpus of the Study ………………………………………… 78
  5.3 Data Gathering Procedures ………………………………… 80
  5.4 Encoding and Decoding of Data …………………………… 82
  5.5 Statistical Instrument ……………………………………… 87

Chapter VI
Distribution of Verbal and Visual Modes …………… 89
  6.1 Functional Distribution of Corpus ………………………… 89
  6.2 Verbal Modes Analysis ……………………………………… 92
  6.3 Visual Modes Analysis ……………………………………… 98

Chapter VII
Meaning-making in Verbal-visual Interaction …… 103
  7.1 Meaning-making in Ideational Function ………………… 103
  7.2 Meaning-making in Interpersonal Function ……………… 113
  7.3 Meaning-making in Interactive Function ………………… 122
  7.4 Interaction Between Verbal and Visual Modes ………… 141
  7.5 Extension on Interpersonal Meaning ……………………… 150
  7.6 Ideology and Power in Visual-verbal Interactions ……… 156

Chapter Ⅷ
Conclusion **162**
    8.1   Contribution of the Study ································ 162
    8.2   Recommendations ·· 166

References ·· 168

Appendices ··· 176

Chapter I

Introduction

1.1 Background of the Study

The modern political system of western societies, whose existence relies on law and order, urges politicians to deal with the conundrums on how to make the public accept their leadership and how to conduct their power and ideology in an amicable way rather than the abusive use of state apparatus. Since human beings are characterized as "linguistic as well as political animals" in essence in philosophy, the art of rhetoric or so-called verbal persuasion, naturally has become the most possible and effective solution to the problem. The Greek polis and the Roman Empire declaring their democracy in politics, "the fulfillment of public service" sometimes depends on "the performance of the orators" (Chilton & Schaffner, 2011). Therefore, discourses should be persuasive in essence, aiming for "some sort of cognitive, emotional or aesthetic effect" (Forceville, 2018). The artificial meaning-making via discourses instead of the resort of violence naturally plays a more decisive role in any social and political practice. Both the 20th and 21st centuries have witnessed great advancement, engagement and combination in two fields. One is the continuous process of political change and reform for democracy, freedom and equality, such as, three waves of world-wide democratization, the feminist movement in western countries, the Civil Rights Movement in the US, the independence movements in the third-world countries and global multi-polarization; the other is the massive expansion and wide application and advancement of mass media, such as newspapers, magazines, televisions, radios and the Internet in the process of political struggle. The truth is that anyone who can have access to the discursive power can dominate such a non-violent process of political reform and movement. Domination and manipulation of discourses have become one of the most prominent features in the western politics. Therefore, the tendency of "turn to discourse" in the 1980s and 1990s helped us to link with frameworks attempting to address links between politics and subjectivity particularly in the use of post-structural theories. Nowadays, linguistic systems in mass media are often mingled or even suspended with information in other signifying systems. Discourse can be signified through both verbal and non-verbal semiotic choices; political discourse can also be regarded as a certain genre of verbal or non-verbal communication dominated by political participants for the implementation of any political intention. In other words, the characteristics of political discourses should be associated with "political actors, political process and political context" not only in the forms of texts but also in other communicative forms (Fairclough & Fairclough, 2012).

In a broad sense, political advertising through mass media belongs to political publicity. Political advertising, "pretended to be a symbol of democracy", appears in systems in which the distribution of political power is contested and determined in elections and in which parties or candidates compete with each other (Kaid & Holtz-Bacha, 2006). Its impact upon political activities and processes cannot be neglected. Studies suggest that political advertising in campaigns of western politics has confirmed its manipulative power in winning over the approval and support from the public in a political election or political propaganda (Devlin, 2001; Kaid & Dimitrova, 2005). Kaid & Holtz-Bacha (2006) claims that political advertising provides this necessary control, allowing candidates and parties to determine the content and style of their messages and take advantage of modern mass-audience channels to maximize the distribution of these promotional messages to potential voters. More significantly, the last several decades have witnessed the change of political propaganda in its form, style and mass media. With the development of the economy and modern technology, the invention of television and its accessibility to every family have led to a revolutionary change in all political activities especially in the campaigns of the US presidential election for its earliest application.

During the 1948 presidential campaign, Harry S. Truman traveled over thirty thousand miles but only shook over half a million hands. Surprisingly, four years later, it was in the year of 1952 that a great success by presidential candidate Dwight D. Eisenhower, the first politician to take advantage of televised campaign advertising in the election all over the world. In his trademarked "no bull" way, these questions collected from the audience were split into televised advertisements and the campaign entitled "Eisenhower Answers America" ran. His performance of bright personality, great leadership, strong decisiveness and iron determination on the screen along with his forceful way in language use, were ultimately responsible for his victory in the election. From then on, Eisenhower's success resulting from his employment of such a new kind of political communication has had great impact on worldwide politics and, naturally, it can merit scholarly attention in different research fields, such as politics, media studies, political communication, stylistics, discourse analysis, etc. With more and more funds poured into televised political advertising year by year, the deliberate design of televised political advertising from all-round information channels can increasingly influence people's way of thinking and understanding effectively. Apparently, activities of western politics rely on the basis of fund input; anyone who is capable of controlling the mass media stands a chance to influence the approval of the public. In other words, western mass media function as the representatives of certain kinds of political circles or interests; the public is possibly affected by them consciously or unconsciously.

1.2 Research Purpose

For its great significance in political activities, studies on televised advertising have been conducted from different academic perspectives, such as politics, media studies, linguistics, etc. Though too much emphasis has been attached on televised political advertising, all the previous researches exclude the following two aspects.

Critical Study

Political advertising apparently being highly socialized and politicalized products, their studies fail to employ a critical perspective on its manipulative power on the voters' ideology and cognition. As a matter of fact, the word "critical" is a dominant term in the field of critical discourse analysis (CDA). To those critical analysts, the purpose of "critical study" principally means unraveling or "denaturalizing" ideologies expressed in discourse and revealing how power structures are constructed and negotiated in and through discourse (Fairclough, 1995, Machin and Mayr, 2012). According to Reisigl and Wodak (2001), "critical" means "not taking things for granted, opening up complexity, challenging reductionism, dogmatism and dichotomies, being self-reflective in my research, and through these processes, making opaque structures of power relations and ideologies manifest". "Critical" does not imply the common sense meaning of "being negative"— rather "skeptical". Therefore, CDA, inspired by functionalism, adopts an interdisciplinary approach to discourse analysis, viewing language as a kind of social practice. Van Dijk (1997) proposes that discourse should not be confined to a form of language use but also treated as a communicative event, in which discourse is closely related to society and cognition. The linguistic theory in CDA has traditionally been drawn upon Halliday's systemic-functional grammar, which is largely concerned with the function of language in the social structure. According to Halliday (1973), the principle function of language is to represent people, objects, events, and states of affairs in the world and to express the speaker's attitude to these representations; language is as it is because of its function in the social structure and discourse is defined as language that is functional. At the same time, CDA treats language as a multifunctional system overlapping with systemic-functional grammar to some degree, which, therefore, is wildly accepted as theoretical foundation and methodology by critical analysts (Kress, 1976; Hodge and Kress, 1993; Iedema, 2003). Both research and theory in systemic-functional linguistics show how linguistic forms can be systematically related to social and ideological functions. In Halliday's Systemic-functional grammar, language, being a social practice, can perform different functions, i. e., it is concerned with the mechanism of text structure, function and meaning of language. For Halliday (1985), language is a "meaning potential". By extension, linguistic study can be defined as "the study of how people exchange meanings by language" (Halliday, 1985). Broadly speaking, as a highly socialized product, language can be roughly and functionally boiled down into two kinds: one is to conduct the performance of social activities; the other is to construct human affiliation within cultures and social groups and institutions. Therefore, in order to understand the social system, its persistence and changes in the course of the transmission of culture from one generation to another, people have to understand the role that language plays in it from a critical point of view. It can be said with certainty that the crafty construction of political discourses in televised political advertising, being a vehicle of political communication, has been treated as one of the most important tools in the implementation of any politics-related intention. In the process of any political activity, it is the discourse that mirrors the internal relationship among language, power and ideology, which is acknowledged to be the focus of CDA.

Multimodal Study

Despite televised political advertising being multi-media creations, analysts neglect taking all the modes into consideration in previous studies as an exclusive and predominant concentration in discourse analysis is given to verbal communication. Cook (1992) stresses that, as a kind of text genre, the most evident characteristic of advertisement is multimodality, namely, the mixture of modes, pictures, music and language. The study on the integration of all the possible semiotic modes, including both verbal and nonverbal ones, has become popular in western countries in 1990, known as Multimodal Discourse Analysis MDA(Kress & Van Leeuwen, 1996). The tendency that the previous studies only center on verbal layer but ignore the function of nonverbal semiotic resources, such as images, gestures, colors, etc., in the process of meaning-making has been altered. The transformation from semiotics to social semiotics made by many scholars (Halliday, 1978; Kress & Van Leeuwen, 1990; Thibault, 1991; Hodge & Kress, 1995; Van Leeuwen, 2005) lays a theoretical foundation for the development of MDA. It was M. A. K Halliday (1978) who first introduced the term "social semiotic" into language study, arguing that the grammar of a language is not a code, not a set of rules for producing correct sentences, but a "resource for making meanings". Kress and Van Leeuwen (1990) analyze meaning-making mechanisms from social semiotics in image. Inspired and guided by the Systemic-Functional Grammar initiated by Halliday (1978), Kress and Van Leeuwen (1996) propose the grammar of visual design in which visual structure, similar to linguistic structure, can point to particular interpretations of experience and forms of interaction. In other words, multimodal discourses in televised political advertising require the merging of more than two modes working together for the meaning-making of the whole discourse.

As a result, study on political discourses should be conducted from a multimodal dimension in a critical way. As Merelman (1986) claims that our knowledge and opinions about politicians, parties or presidents are largely acquired, changed or confirmed by various forms of texts and talks during our socialization, formal education, media usage and conversation, political information processing is often a form of discourse processing, because much of the political action and participation is accomplished by discourse and communication. Television provides a multimedia platform for information transmission. Therefore, with the aim of arousing the audience's interests and enhancing the objectivity, authenticity and persuasiveness in political discourses, the proper design of televised political advertising may greatly influence the audience's perception, cognition, comprehension and decision, further assists the politicians in achieving certain political objectives, as language use along with the exaggerated artistic creations such as image composition, background music, coloring and presentation of identities may cognitively influence the recognition of potential supporters. Obviously, similar to the verbal modes, all the other modes in televised political advertising must be ideological, functioning as the way social power abuse, dominance and inequality are enacted, reproduced, and resisted in a social and political context.

For such a reason, Kress and Van Leeuwen (1996) emphasize that the analysis of visual communication should be an indispensable component of "critical" disciplines, in which imagines of whatever kind as entirely within the realm of the realizations and instantiations of ideology. Visual Grammar can be regarded as a "broadened critical discourse analysis" (Kress & Van Leeuwen, 1996). Machin and Mayr (2012) propose a completely new approach of MCDA that regards all the modes of communication, both verbal and visual semiotics, as a means of social construction. MCDA is not so much interested in the visual semiotic choices in themselves, but also in the way that they play a part in the communication of power relations. MCDA, an extension of CDA to multimodal studies, can expose strategies that appear normal or neutral on the surface but which may in fact seek to ideologically shape the representation of events and persons, for particular ends in televised political advertising.

The electoral system is an important part of the political system of modern countries and it is widely recognized as a foundation of legitimate government. It is through the electoral system that modern countries show their recognition of democratic politics and respect for civil rights. Theoretically, political elections having strong operability can directly express the will of the people; hence it is widely adopted by most western countries and political communities. By persuading citizens to choose the manner in which they are governed, elections form the starting point for all other democratic institutions and practices. America being the most powerful country all over the world, its presidential election, a quadrennial political gala, is a typical representation of US political system attracting worldwide attention. As the presidency is determined by the voters, the presidential candidates have to grasp or create enough opportunities, such as talk shows, presidential debates, political advertising and the like, to make positive self-representation on the one hand and negative other-representation on the other hand, so as to obtain the favor and support of the public as possible as they can. Among the marketing instruments at a campaign's disposal, statistics indicate that the employment of campaign advertising has both grown in importance and prevalence over the past few decades. For example, during the presidential election in 2012, both campaigns and their supporters aired more than 1.1 million TV advertising (Wesleyan Media Project, 2012; *Washington Post*, 2012).

For the sake of the significance of campaign advertising in the American presidential election, the present study focuses on the collection and analysis of US presidential election campaign advertising in three election cycles from 2008 to 2016 as a case study from the perspective of social semiotics. The combination of both qualitative and quantitative approaches can ensure the scientificity and objectivity and facilitate the study. Based on the functional classifications of the data proposed by Benoit (1996), the results will be analyzed and discussed from two different perspectives, namely, verbal and visual. The corresponding techniques will be used: SPSS for data calculation in functional analysis, Antconc3.2.1 for the study on language use and PotPlayer 64 bit for capture of different images. Adopting Benoit's functional approach to political advertising, the present study firstly classifies 206 pieces of US General Election Campaign Advertising into two categories: positive and negative advertising, with its attention on the participants in discourses. Then, the main framework of Halliday's Systemic-Functional

Grammar and its subsequent amendment and complement will be used for the analysis of verbal level, including both oral (transcript) and textual content. Kress & Van Leeuwen's Visual Grammar is used for the analysis of visual level and Machin & Mayr's analytical methods and tools are used to build an integrated model for MCDA which consists of vocal (non-linguistic sound system) mode analysis, verbal mode analysis, visual mode analysis and the interaction among those modes. Van Dijk's socio-cognitive approach to discourse can be used as reference to the discussion on manipulation of public cognition.

1.3 Significance of the Research

The study on televised political advevtising has great theoretical significance. Firstly, though a thorough diachronic study has been conducted to American General Election Campaign Advertising from 1952 to 2000 (Benoit, 2000; Benoit, 2003), its function-based study on political advertising is still restricted to mono-mode in terms of its content, topic and themes. Thus, a small-scale data analysis of various semiotic modes in US General Election Campaign advertising from 2008 to 2016 can be regarded as an indispensable supplement to the previous study, which can greatly enrich Benoit's functional approach to televised political advertising. In addition, this study contributes to the improvement and refinement of analysis framework of multimodal critical studies in political discourse.

Meanwhile, the study also has practical significance. Political advertising has its own special characteristics in the process of meaning-making. Its highly distinctive features in choices of words, syntactic construction, rhetoric features and diversification may be deceptive and misleading to the public. The exposures of the latent relationship of power, ideology and different kinds of modes in televised political advertising can cultivate critical awareness, helping to make rational judgments without being dizzied and misled by the flood of multimodal information. Therefore, this study could improve people's semiotic awareness and reshape their outlook upon the discourses of political advertising.

1.4 Statement of the Problems

On the basis of functional classifications of political advertising (positive and negative advertising) and collection of the corpus of televised US general election campaign advertising, the study tries to answer the following questions:
  (1) How are verbal modes employed in televised political advertising from the perspective of ideational and interpersonal function in SFG?
  (2) How are visual modes employed in televised political advertising from the perspective of interactive meaning in Visual Grammar?
  (3) How do the verbal and visual modes interact with one another to show power and ideology in televised political advertising?

Regarding the realization of two different functions, namely, positive or negative, the purpose of this corpus-based study aims to explore the distribution of multimodality in political advertising, to discuss the correlation and interaction among those co-existing modes, and to explore the outstanding strategies used by politicians for better manipulating the thoughts of the public in its complexity of those semiotic resources. Finally, it fundamentally aims to enhance the semiotic awareness of the public through the analysis of multimodal semiotic choices made by the producers, revealing power interests buried in various modes.

Chapter II

Review of Related Literature

According to Van Leeuwen (2013), the term "critical analysis of multimodal discourse" suggests "a merger of two distinct fields of applied linguistics: critical discourse analysis and multimodality". In order to better expand the research into a large scale, this part theoretically focuses on the socio-cultural orientation of CDA and MCDA from two perspectives, namely, social semiotics foundation and Sapir-Whorf Hypothesis. Then, a brief introduction to the evolution of theories in the light of the studies in social semiotics and the exemplifications of correlated terms will be made.

2.1 Social Semiotic Foundation

The term semiotics or semiology, originating from ancient Greek, means the study of signs. The semiotic tradition explores the study of signs and symbols as a significant part of communication. Stubbes (1676) firstly illustrates the term of semiology in a precise sense to denote the branch of medical science relating to the interpretation of signs. The theoretical framework of modern semiotics was established at the beginning of the 20th century, owing to the great contributions made by Ferdinand de Saussure, who is also considered to be the pioneer of structuralism in the study of semiotics.

Being the forefather of both modern linguistics and semiotics, Saussure (1915, 1974) regards semiotics as "the science of life of signs in society". In this term, everything in a culture can be seen as a form of communication, organized in ways akin to verbal language, to be understood in terms of a common set of fundamental rules and principles (Hodge & Kress, 1988). He treats linguistic study as a part of semiotics and proposes the dyadic model of "linguistic sign" consisting of "signifier" and "signified", holding that the relationship between the signified and signifier is arbitrary, as there is no natural relationship between the object and sound system to the object (Saussure, 1974). The ideas, central to his linguistic conception, lead to the advent of modern linguistics, considering language as an object of study that needs to be studied in itself. Saussure proposes that:

> Language is a system of signs that express ideas, and is therefore comparable to a system of writing, the alphabet of deaf-mutes, symbolic rites, polite formulas, military signals, etc. But it is the most important of all these systems. (1916)

In other words, language can be regarded as an arbitrary system of signs. For example, there is no direct referential but relational relationship between the numbers on the button in the elevator and the floors they refer to. Being one of the pioneers of structuralism, his proposal of a social, systemic and structural perspective on semiotics with linguistic signs as its focus lays the foundation for the future study on linguistics and semiotics.

Apparently, the arbitrariness of semiotics requires a certain social and cultural mechanism shared in a certain language community that can facilitate communication among its users. Language, part of semiotics, is regarded as a conventional process of encoding and decoding in which the relationship between signified and signifiers is constructed by social practice and social cognition.

In addition, Saussure defines the two major contrary concepts—langue and parole. "Langue" is an underlying system which is common in speech or utterance, while "parole" is an individual's speech and has complete or partial social acceptability. For the concept of "langue" and "parole", their

Chapter II Review of Related Literature

paradigmatic and syntagmatic relationship is added by Saussure with the classification of language-study into two sections: diachronic and synchronic.

In spite of the indispensable social factors in his dichotomy in semiotic study, his focus on the study of the signifier instead of the signified and his preference for the synchronic instead of diachronic approach led to the inclination to the study of the relation of symbolic system but the neglect of symbol meaning itself in structuralism. In addition, his emphasis on the patterns, systems and structures of language instead of its meaning and usage also obliterates the sociality of language. Under his influence, for instance, the post structural US linguist, Chomsky claims that the human brain is especially constructed to detect and reproduce language. According to Chomsky, children instinctively apply innate grammatical rules to process the verbal input to which they are exposed.

Afterwards, the limitation of Saussure's dichotomic concept of "sign" was challenged and amended in the course of time for the rigidity and constraints of signifier and signified, "splitting process from product, subject from structure" (Coward & Ellis, 1977). The one to one, non-inherent relationship between the "signifier" or "sound image" and "concept" or "object" has been challenged by the structural critic and theorist(Barthes, 1973). Though insisting on being a structuralist, Barthes (1973) extends his concept of "sign"—"signifier" and "signified" in order to emancipate the rigidity between the components of a "sign". He calls it firstness of meaning, i.e. "denotation". The signified has associative or connotative meanings, which are numberless and dependent on contexts.

The emphasis on the importance of contexts in communication leads to the change of semiotic study. Enlightened by the Malinowski anthropological semantics in the study of context in meaning, Firth (1930) and Halliday (1978) as the representatives, propose and develop the concept ofcontextualism. According to Halliday (1978), the context situation in which language is used is defined as register, including "field of discourse (setting)" "tenor of discourse (relationship between participants)" and "mode of discourse (channel of communication)". To put it simple, register is characterized by "differences in the type of language selected as appropriate to different types of situation" (Halliday, et. al. 1964), which means that there is a close relationship between language and context of the situation. The introduction and evolution of contextualism into the study of signs indicates four transformations in semiotic study: from traditional semiotics to social semiotics, from semantics to pragmatics, from linguistic study as its focus to the combination of verbal and visual signs and from structuralism to functionalism. For example, the design of modern public mass media, such as newspapers, magazines, and the like on political activities co-exist organization of various signs in a certain way. The study of the stylistics on those political discourses should not only be confined to the linguistic study itself but also be extended to the demonstration of the meaning-making process of all signs, taking the historical, cultural, social and political elements into consideration.

Halliday (1978) criticizes "traditional semiotics" for its extreme attention to structures and codes at the expense of functions and social uses of semiotic systems meanwhile inheriting its thoughts on the sociality of language which has been verified but ignored by Saussure. Contrary to the contemporary theory of formalism like behaviorism with its focus on structure rather than semantics in language study (Bloomfield, 1993) and Chomsky's generative grammar with its focus on linguistic competence (Chomsky, 1957), the explanation of different linguistic choices in language use is not a puzzlement in form but also a choice in meaning-making regarding to the functions it performs in society. Halliday (1978) regards language as the encoding of a "behavior potential" into a "meaning potential". More precisely, being a branch of semiotics, or its new research orientation, social semiotics focuses on the generation of meaning through a certain system of signs in specific social and cultural circumstances, and regards meaning-making as a social practice. It studies the media of dissemination and the modes of communication that people use and develop to represent their understanding of the world and to shape power relations with others. Jewitt and Oyama (2001) note that social semiotics is "not an

Chapter Ⅱ Review of Related Literature

end itself but a tool for use in critical study". In other words, the fact that a variety of linguistic and semiotic choices depend on the roles that they play in the construction and maintenance of social affiliations under different social contexts needs to be exposed in social semiotic study. Hodge and Kress (1988) also criticize Saussure's option for considerations of value (relation in system), signification rather than reference. Inspired by Halliday's theory of social semiotics, Hodge and Kress(1988), aiming to establish a whole heartedly "social semiotics", extend the general framework beyond its linguistic origins to account for the growing importance of sound and visual images and declare that social semiotics cannot assume "that texts produce exactly the meanings and effects that their authors hope for: it is precisely the struggles and their uncertain outcomes that must be studies at the level of social action, and their effects in the production of meaning". Just as Thibault (1991) proposes that the study of social semiotics aims to develop theoretical and analytical frameworks that can explain meaning-making in a social context, the study of any sign is the study of social behavior through meaning per se, as the speaker has the potential to act what he or she "can do", which is also technologically called "meaning potential". In other words, its potentiality lies in the totality of meanings conventionally expressed by and through a given semiotic resource to achieve certain communicative effects. In terms of the possible functions of language realized in the social activities, Halliday (1975) argues that no arbitrariness exists between semantics and syntax. Therefore, study of social semiotics should attach great importance to the enactment of social activities in terms of the construction of semiotic meanings dominated by social, cultural and ideological factors hidden in discourse practices. For this matter, Halliday's theory of social semiotics lays the foundation for the development of both CDA and MCDA. On the one hand, Halliday's emphasis on social properties in the choice of linguistic semiotics in meaning-making complies with the concentration on the exploration of ideological and manipulative dominance in language use in CDA; on the other hand, the emphasis on meaning-making in social practice results in a fresh look at social semiotic study, that is, the expansion of its focus ranging from the linguistic signs to non-linguistic signs in the implementation of meaning potential. Halliday and Matthiessen (1999) propose that socio-semiotic systems that are parasitic on language, in the sense that they depend on the fact that those who use them are articulate ("linguale") beings. To this extent, language, being a kind of semiotics, can express and construct social structure and system at the same time, and this expression and construction is not limited to the language itself, but also in all aspects of culture consisting of many symbolic systems, such as architecture, art, dance, music, literature, folklore, etiquette, commodity exchange and so on. In other words, how those different semiotic resources are chosen and assembled in meaning making can determine the communication of ideas, values, and identities and constrain different kinds of interactions. The crucial implication here is that meanings and semiotic systems are shaped by social structures, and that as social structures shift in society, our languages and other systems of socially accepted meanings can and do change.

2.2 Sapir-Whorf Hypothesis

The knowledge-based view of culture can be regarded as a cognitive view, because of its focus on the principally mental organization of reality. Semiologists illustrate culture in a semiotic way, focusing on interpretation process and meaning (Keating & Durabnti, 2011). Study on culture should link people with objects in their environment. Therefore, culture cannot be neglected in the construction of social practice. The Sapir-Whorf hypothesis refers to the proposal that the particular language one speaks influences the way one thinks about reality. Linguistic relativity stands in close relation to semiotic-level concerns with the general relation of language and thought, and to discourse-level concerns with how patterns of language use in cultural context can affect thought. Linguistic relativity is distinguished both from simple linguistic diversity and from strict linguistic determinism. They argue

Chapter Ⅱ   Review of Related Literature

that our perception of reality varies according to the language that we speak, and that "real world" is to a large extent built up on the language habits of the group. Though their theory is still controversial and much debated, the influence of language upon thought is obvious.

In its strong form, which is called linguistic determinism, it rules out the possibility that people may engage in "linguistic engineering"—manipulating language to thought, while in terms of the weak form, it clings to the fact that linguistic engineers will not always succeed in achieving their aims. Though few linguists accept the strong form, what the speakers say will inevitably have a wondrous influence on your thoughts, but by no means determine them.

This hypothesis concerning cultural influence upon social practice has become the foundation of sociolinguistics. It is adopted in CDA and first adapted in *Language and Control* (1979) as "varying choices of words and constructions within one language" expresses different or contrasting "analyses and assessments in specific areas of experience: not total world views, but specialized systems of ideas relevant to events". The point here is that different linguistic structures reflect different systems of ideas or ideologies. In social struggle, contending forces may use radically different linguistic strategies to depict the same social events manipulating people to see the world as intended. Thus linguistic variation has much to do with social meanings. In addition, the social context along with the language use jointly influences one's cognition of the physical and mental world. For the critical linguistic analysts, the creation and measurement of the force in wording has been one of the focuses in CDA. Therefore, the belief in Sapir-Whorf Hypothesis is also regarded as one of the theoretical foundations in CDA, emphasizing the dominant influence of language upon one's cognition. With CDA framework, controlling people's thoughts through the choice of words, rhetoric features and so on, is one of the fundamental ways to reproduce power, dominance and hegemony in social contexts. Machin and Mayr (2012) claim that the employment of certain language in certain setting results from "social pressures rather than linguistic determinism". For example, a housewife may persuade her husband not smoking by saying "No smoking", while for a piece of public service advertising in the hospital, the prohibition of smoking may appear like an imperative sentence "NO SMOKING". Obviously, the influence of the two sentences upon the receiver is different because of their differentiations in sentence construction. The former one employed by a housewife, the husband may commonly give his excuses to smoke at home, ignorant of his wife's request. The latter one, placed in a public place, can influence the behavior of the smokers cognitively for the imperative sentence structure has strong dominant force imposing to those who try to smoke in hospital though both the linguistic modes and visual modes have the same meaning.

As mentioned above, the concept of "sign" can be understood from two perspectives, linguistics and semiotics. In linguistics, "language" is the focal point of study. In semiotics, "sign" is the basic and distinctive unit of study. The characteristics and functions associated with language are also applicable to "signs" used in communication. From an empirical perspective, such influence of semiotic choices in linguistics can be found in the multimodal field of communication as well. Three colors of the traffic lights established by regulations and conventions can be the best exemplification. It is a set of universally conventional rules in which the color of red means to stop, green means to move and yellow means to be cautious. The distinction between linguistic determinism and linguistic relativity can also be practical. On one hand, the restriction of the red color on a person's behavior is dominant on the road; on the other hand, the prohibition is relatively context-based, because the meaning-making of the three colors is only applicable in the public places and to those who can distinguish the colors. Here is the public service advertising on smoking which can further expose the semiotic relativity and semiotic determinism on the receivers:

Chapter Ⅱ Review of Related Literature

Figure 1 Cognitive Recognition of Cigarette Advertising

On the cigarette boxes, the capitalization of all the letters in the word "warning" is apparently unnecessary from linguistic perspective but is cognitively attractive to the consumers. In addition, the noticeable cigarettes above together with the crying woman and the dying man below construct a complete interpretation of the harmful consequences of smoking. Naturally, the influence towards the smokers' behavior is proved to be more effective than the purely linguistic form like "Cigarettes cause strokes and heart disease". It is apparent that such a deliberate multimodal design can gradually reduce the habits of smoking as it can consolidate the awareness of risks resulting from smoking, because smoking can cause fatal diseases. Though it can be said with certainty that the delivery of meaning through multimodality is a more efficient and explicit way, its influence upon the receiver's actions is not absolute, as not every smoker stops smoking because of the special design on the package of cigarettes. Just as Machin and Mayr (2012) propose that communication in language is based, as in the Sapir-whorf model, on the idea that "everyone agrees to use the same words to mean the same thing", no natural relationship exists between what you say and what you mean but "a concept can be established by the people through long social practice". A conclusion can be arrived here that the influence in verbal mode in Sapir-whorf Hypothesis can be extended to a large scale in non-verbal mode, because in the process of meaning production and perception they have the same mechanism in which the producers, abiding by certain cultural and contextual conventions or rules, can make and understand reasonable semiotic choices in social interactions, which can be understood by the receivers.

2.3 From CDA to MCDA

Discursive practice takes us through "turn to language" and "turn to discourse" to a conception of language as materially effective. The turn to language in psychology in the late 1960s and 1970s shifted attention to aspects of human activity that were neglected by traditional psychology. Then the "turn to discourse" in the 1980s and 1990s helped us to link with frameworks attempting to address links between politics and subjectivity particularly in the use of post-structural theories. While most linguists concentrate on the formal aspects of language which constitute the linguistic competence of speakers and which could theoretically be isolated from specific instances of language use, as the mainstream of linguistic research (Chomsky, 1957). In the late 1970s, Critical Linguistics, a form of discourse and text analysis, was developed by a group of linguists and literary theorists at the University of East Anglia, recognizing the role of language in structuring power relations in society with its first appearance in *Language and Control*, written by Roger Fowler. The notion of CDA appeared in Norman Fairclough's *Language and Power* published in 1989. Different critical discourse analysts, such as Kress and Hodge (1979), Fowler et al. (1979), Van Dijk (1985), Fairclough (1989) and Wodak (1989), give an account of the definition, the theoretical foundations, corpus as well as its research methodology of CDA from their own perspectives. The terms critical linguistics and critical discourse analysis are often used interchangeably. In recent times, it seems that the term CDA is preferred.

Being the forefather of critical linguistics, Kress (1990) elaborates on the theoretical foundations and sources of critical linguistics. Kress (1990) shows how CDA by that time was "emerging as a distinct theory of language, a radically different kind of linguistics. Meanwhile, he lays down the criteria that distinguish the aim of other forms of discourse analysis from

Chapter Ⅱ Review of Related Literature

CDA. The most outstanding contribution made by Kress is the following basic assumptions of CDA which were salient in the early ages:

Language is a social phenomenon.

Not only individuals, but also institutions and social groupings have specific meanings and values, which are expressed in language in systematic ways;

Texts are the relevant units of language in communication;

Readers/hearers are not passive recipients in their relationship to texts;

There are similarities between the language of science and the language of institutions, and so on. (1989)

In later development, his research interest turned to the "political economy of representational media which aims at understanding how various societies value different modes of representation, and how they use these different modes of representation. So far, much of Kress's effort has gone into thinking about the content of educational curricula in terms of representational resources and their use by individuals in their constant transformation of their subjectivities, the process usually called "learning".

Van Dijk makes great contribution to the development of CDA in critical studies of media discourse. According to Van Dijk (2001), CDA is a type of discourse analytical research that primarily studies the way that social power abuse, dominance and inequality are enacted, reproduced, and resisted by text and talk in social and political context. Van Dijk(1995)treats discourse analysis as ideology analysis in essence as he holds that ideology is typically, though not exclusively, expressed and reproduced in discourse and communication, including visual semiotic messages, such as pictures, photographs and movies.

What distinguishes Van Dijk's framework for the analysis of media discourse is his call for a thorough analysis not only for the textual and structural level of media discourse but also for analysis and explanations at the production and "reception" or comprehension level (Boyd-Barrent, 1994). He attaches great importance to the structural analysis on which he insists that description at various levels of structures should be made, including not only the grammatical, phonological and semantic level but also coherence, overall themes, the whole schematic forms and rhetorical dimensions of texts. As for "production process", he means journalistic and institutional practices of news-making and economic and social practices which play important roles in the design of media discourse. In addition, the process of semiotic production can be explicitly related to the structures of media course. In terms of his "reception process", he claims that comprehension, memorization and reproduction should be taken into account.

Another great achievement is his application of the psycho-cognitive model into CDA. The theory in early period of CDA has been greatly influenced by Hallidayan systematic-functional grammar, Marxism and post-structuralism while Van Dijk particularly focuses on the fruits of psycholinguistics and cognitive linguistics. He asserts the influence of cognitive model upon the structures of discourses and texts and the relationship between human mentalities, context models and social structures which will be elaborated more in the methodology of this thesis. Generally speaking, his analysis of ideology consists of three parts, namely, social analysis, cognitive analysis and discourse analysis: The social analysis pertains to the context; the discourse analysis needs to be text-based and cognitive analysis should include social cognition and personal cognition. To some extent, the most outstanding feature of his approach, compared with other approaches in CDA, is his cognitive analysis. For Van Dijk it is the above-mentioned two kinds of cognitions meditating between society and discourse, known as sociocognition. He claims that his general framework is a multidisciplinary brand of CDA that tries to "triangulate" social issues in terms of a combined study of discursive, cognitive, and social dimensions of a problem (Van Dijk, 1993). Consequently, while doing critical researches on the features of political speeches, such as political advertising, it is not enough to restrict them into description but to extend them into a larger scale—the explanation of text or discourse by linking them to the following socio-cognitive representation, for instance, attitudes, norms, values and ideologies, etc.

Chapter II Review of Related Literature

Fairclough (1993) defines CDA as a systematic exploration on the opaque relationships of causality and determination between discursive practices, events and texts, and wider social and cultural structures, relations and processes. He defines the research scope of critical study and elaborates his famous three-dimensional model of CDA which is applicable for use in the sort of research into social and cultural change affected by language or vice versa. In particular, it foregrounds the links between social practice and language and the systematic investigation of connections between the nature of social processes and properties of language texts (Fairclough, 1995). According to the diagram, it can be roughly divided into two parts with their own segments: one is the dimensions of discourse and the other is dimension of discourse analysis as shown in the following diagram, which is known as the framework for CDA of both written and spoken language (ibid).

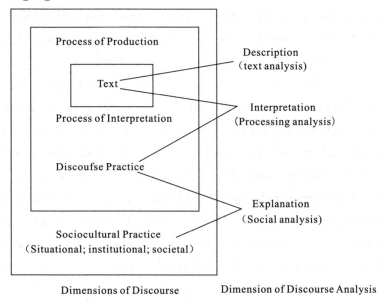

Figure 2 Fairclough's Dimensions of Discourse Analysis

When analyzing any discourse, Fairclough's technique of CDA includes three different but interrelated dimensions, namely, a language text (spoken or written), discourse practice (text production and text interpretation) and sociocultural practice(text, whether it be written or spoken, referring to various genres of linguistic materials, such as, news reports, political speeches, even short conversations) as Fairclough (1995) claims that a spoken "text" can of course be turned into a written text by transcription; discourse practice referring to text production and text interpretation and sociocultural practice with three different levels, namely, situational level, institutional level and societal level. As for the dimension of discourse analysis, it involves three steps in the whole process of discourse analysis including the linguistic description of text, referring to the linguistic analysis of the language text in terms of vocabulary, grammar, semantics, the sound system and cohesion, interpretation of the relationship between the discursive process and the text and explanation of the relationship between the discursive process and social process. According to the second Figure, it is clear that the relationship between linguistic text and sociocultural practice is mediated by discourse practice. Therefore, how a text is produced and interpreted, on one hand, is determined by the nature of sociocultural practice, which determines how the surface features (linguistic features) of a text will be analyzed on the other hand. To some extent, Fairclough's three-dimensional model sees language as a multi-functional system. It is grounded on Hallidayan Systemic-Functional Grammar, the metafunction; his three layers of critical analysis correspond to ideational function, interpersonal function and textual function (Wang Qingxin & Ji Weining, 2000).

Wodak constructs her theory on the Hallidayan linguistics, sociolinguistics in the Bernsteinian tradition, and the ideas of the Frankfurt school, especially given by Foucault, Bakhtin and Voloshinov. She supports the suggestion of other critical linguistics who believe that relationships between language and society are so complex and multifaceted that interdisciplinarity is required (2000).

Her researches are expanded into various institutional settings, such as hospitals, courts and schools, and a variety of social issues like sexism, racism and anti-semitism. For a better explanation and interpretation of discourses in various social situations, Wodak proposes a historical study of contexts in CDA which distinguishes her approach from those of other critical linguistic analysts. Her focus on the necessity of a historical perspective in CDA develops into a new approach termed as the discourse-historical method, which denotes an attempt on the part of this approach "to systematically integrate all available background information in the analysis and interpretation of the many layers of a written or spoken text" (1995). In the practice of such an approach, Wodak (1999) finds the great impact of context of the discourse upon its structure and function and believes that language "manifests social processes and interaction" and "constitutes" those processes.

Though various research methodologies and orientations are adopted in CDA, it can be concluded that the core of the study focuses on the internal relationship among discourse practices, social practices and social structure. Based on the explanations mentioned above, several conclusions about theoretical and analytical basis in this field can be arrived:

Firstly, it adopts the theory of post-structuralism that discourse operates laterally across local institutional sites and that text has a constructive function in building, shaping and keeping human identities and actions. Under the guidance of Hallidayan systemic-functional grammar in which "language is regarded as means of expressing what the human organism 'can do', in interaction with other human organisms, by turning it into what 'he can mean'" (Halliday, 1978), the core of CDA focuses on the internal relationship among discourse practices, social practices and social structure. In other words, the use of language can be regarded as a form of social practice in which language both shapes society and is shaped by the society. CDA conducts social analysis from the perspective of linguistics. It integrates language analysis with social analysis. Unlike the pure concentration on discourse study itself in structuralism, it aims to expose the underlying social phenomenon and problems, such as inequality, hegemony, discrimination and the like, which are buried in the use of language.

Secondly, another central term in CDA is power. Van Dijk claims that one of the crucial tasks of CDA is to account for the relationships between discourse and social power. As power is defined as a property of relations between social groups, institutions or organizations, the research target in CDA, more precisely, should be constraint in the study of social power rather than individual power. According to Van Dijk (1993), one crucial presupposition of adequate CDA is "understanding the nature of social power and dominance". Concerning the definition of power, Xin (2005) divides its conception into two categories: one refers to one's capacity of pursuing his/her interests or goals, known as power-to; the other refers to one's ability of controlling other people, known as power-over. Fairclough (1995) explains that the significance of power in discourse studies lies in "its asymmetries between participants in discourse events and the unequal capacity to control the production, distribution and consuming of the texts in a particular socio-cultural contexts". Therefore, the accessibility to power and the abuse of power should be taken into consideration in the whole process of discourse analysis. Obviously, western political elections being unbalanced distribution of power for its monetary reason, not all people have the equal opportunity to get access to the media or to medical, legal, political, bureaucratic or scholarly text and talk. Therefore, the measures of accessibility to discourse may be rather faithful indicators of the power of social groups and their members (Van Dijk, 1996). The unbalanced situation in discourse power distribution naturally leads to unfairness, control and dominance in social and political life.

Thirdly, the term "ideology" is the other central term in critical discourse studies. It draws from Neo-Marxist cultural theory—the assumption that these discourses are produced and used within political economies, and that they thus produce and articulate broader ideological interests, social formations and movements within those fields (Althusser, 1979). In Marxism, ideologies are forms of "false consciousness" or "false belief". Those ideologies are popular but misguided beliefs imposed by the dominant class. However, with critical linguistics, ideology is not considered as "false consciousnesses or false belief" but treated as the way that the ideas and values that comprise these ideas on the way the world works. Its first

Chapter II Review of Related Literature

incorporation with semiotic study was made by Voloshinov, claiming that "everything ideological possesses meaning: it represents, depicts, or stands for something lying outside itself" (1973). Supposing that meaning must be expressed with signs in human communication as its arbitrariness of the signifier and the signified, no ideological expression can exist without signs. Every phenomenon function as an ideological sign has some kind of "material embodiment, whether in sound, physical mass, color, movement of the body, and the like" (Voloshinov, 1973). Critical linguists have offered a more neutral kind of definition of ideology: the way in which people think, say, and interact with the society. In CDA, taken as an important aspect of establishing and maintaining unequal power relation in discourse, ideologies are the basic framework for organizing the social cognitions shared by members of social groups, organizations or institutions. According to Van Dijk (1995), the point of ideological discourse analysis is not merely to "discover underlying ideologies, but to systematically link structures of discourse with structure of ideologies, for the purpose of exploring how ideological discourses serve to sustain or change social positions". Being the fundamental social cognition that reflects the basic aim, interests and values of groups, ideologies are both cognitive and social. They essentially, function as the interface between the cognitive representations and process underlying discourse and action. "Linguistic forms allow significance to be conveyed and to be distorted." (Kress & Hodge, 1979). Linguistic variation is an indicator of ideological variation.

Though more and more scholars are becoming engaged in critical discourse studies, on the basis of the above-mentioned analysis on the development of their theories and research methodology CDA, there are four main schools in this field, illustrated below.

Table 1　Main Schools of Research on CDA

Research Background	Leading Figure
The social semiotics	Kress and Van Leeuwen
The social-cognitive approach	T. A. Van Dijk
The theory of social change of the Lancaster	Norman Fairclough
The discourse-historical approach	Ruth Wodak

It is clear that CDA aims to "capture the interrelationship between language, power and ideology and especially to draw out and describe the practices and conventions in and behind texts" (Machin & Mayr, 2012). The problem is that it mainly focuses on the relationship between the linguistic system and the semantic structure itself and its relationship with the social culture and the psychological cognition, but often neglects other signs, such as image, sound, color, animation and so on in meaning (Zhu, 2007). However, the constant study of the different semiotic resources of communication has confirmed that monotonous linguistic signs are not effective and efficient enough to achieve certain communicative purposes in different social contexts. Other forms of signs expressed and perceived by human beings with five sensory channels, including visual sensory, auditive sensory, tactile sensory, olfactory sensory and gustatory sensory can also be treated as complement or necessity to construct a complex of information transfer. For example, Semaphore flags, are commonly used as transmission of communication in mountainous areas or in the maritime world where oral or electronic communication is difficult to perform.

2.4　Modes Contributing to Meaning-making

Kress and Van Leeuwen (2001) regard mode, as the semiotic resources, which can realize the discourse and communication type at the same time. It should be noted that great confusion exists among the terms of mode or modality and media, a more familiar term to the public should be clarified first. The figure below indicates that information flow is an encoding and decoding process of the content from different sources to users through different channels of communication.

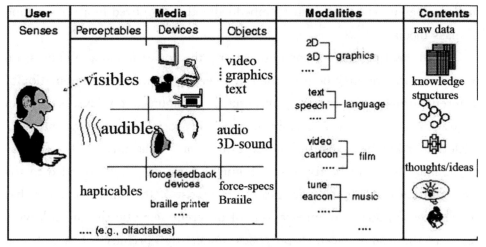

Figure 3 Channels of Communication

According to Figure 3, it can be figured out that the modality or mode refers to different communicative resources or mechanisms in which the source information (content) is embedded, such as film, music, language, graphs and the like. In other words, modes can be regarded as expressive forms of information which need to be encoded and decoded by the speakers and hears. However, the media can be regarded as the collective communication outlets that are used to store and convey information or data, such as CD-Rom, computer, print media and the press, photography, advertising, cinema, broadcasting (radio and television) and publishing. In addition, some authors seem to use both terms as synonyms, while others tend to reserve modality only for input (to be processed by a machine interpreter), and vice versa, media only for output (to be produced by a machine generator).

For some scholars, the terms of modality and mode can be used interchangeably (Lemake, 2003; O'Halloran, 2004; Constantinou, 2005). Lemake (2003) comments that it is this essential incommensurability that enables genuine new meanings to be made from the combinations of modalities. The present study adopts neutral attitudes towards them, considering that modes and media are different but indivisible. Though its research targets, such as words, sounds and images are regarded as semiotic modes, they must be inherently embedded and transmitted in a certain kind of mass media.

In the real practice of communication, the construction and expression of certain meaning may be presented in a certain form or the combination of different forms with the same meaning in communication (Kress & Van Leeuwen, 2001). For a certain purpose of social interaction, namely, "deletion, addition, substitution and evaluation" (Machin, 2013), the use of the language can't be fixed in a linguistic form only but extended to the collaboration with other semiotic resources most of the time. It is clear that the choices, options and integrations of different semiotic resources largely rely on the communicative purposes under the premise of social and contextual conditions. As for the importance of the differences between the various mass media in the channels and technologies they draw upon, Norman Fairclough(1995) comments that:

> The press uses a visual channel, its language is written, and it draws upon technologies of photographic reproduction, graphic design, and printing. Radio, by contrast, uses an oral channel and spoken language and relies on technologies of sound recording and broadcasting, whilst television combines technologies of sound- and image-recording and broadcasting.

These differences in channel and technology have significant wider implications in terms of the meaning-potential of the different media. For instance, print is, in an important sense, less personal than radio ortelevision. Radio begins to allow individuality and personality to be more grounded through transmitting individual qualities of voice. Television takes the process much further by making people visually available, and not in the frozen modality of newspaper photographs, but in movement and action.

With the recent advancement of modern technology, more and more dimensions of semiotic resources are possible to be integrated into the process of meaning-making, which has aroused great interest in social semiotic study. Multimodality first appeared in linguistic study through the groundbreaking work of Kress and Van Leeuwen in *Reading Images* (1996, 2006) and *Multimodal Discourse* (2001). The compound word "multimodality" literally indicates "multi" pluses "modality", meaning more than one modes function as the resources of communication. This term, over the past 20 years, has been taken up by linguists and discourse analysts to denote the integration of different communicative resources, such as language, image, sound and music, in multimodal texts and communicative events (Van Leeuwen, 2013). Other experts also explain the term. Iedema (2003) proposes that the introduction of multimodality aims "to emphasize the importance of taking into account semiotics other than language-in-use, such as image, music, gesture and so on". Technically, it aims to highlight that the meaning work we do at all times exploits various semiotics (Iedema, 2003). Baldry & Thibault (2006) define multimodality as the diverse ways in which a number of distinct semiotic resource systems are both co-deployed and co-contextualized in the making of a text-specific meaning. Multimodality therefore describes the grammar of both verbal and visual communication adopted by the communicators. It is an analysis of the rules and principles that allows viewers to understand the meaning potential of the relative placement of elements, framing, salience proximity, color saturations, styles of typeface, etc. (Machin, 2007). These definitions define multimodality as multimodal systems being extensions of propositional logic whose language is equipped with one or more non-truth-functional operators that are interpretable via some sort of semantics, such as relational semantics.

As a matter of fact, even for the seemingly mono-modal linguistic form in the book, its different colors and font size may imply different meanings. In addition, the change of pitch and tone in oral communication may be perceived and understood by the hearers. To some extent, all the communications are multimodal rather than mono-modal per se; therefore, the study of discourse should include all the modes of meaning-making and fix on the internal relationship among them. For example, the theme of admiration for others can be expressed in a simple word "great" in written or spoken form, a gesture with a thumbs-up, a direct eye contact with fondness, a bunch of colorful flowers or a short film whose content is related to admiration. Whether it is mono-modality or multi-modality depends on the speakers' purposeful choices of those resources to express the same theme simultaneously and their interaction with the audience in a social and contextual context. It is common that at least two semiotic resources are adopted with the word "great" and "a thumbs-up". In other words, the term "mode" referring to different forms of information can be roughly classified into two categories with their own subsets: one is the verbal modes, namely, linguistic signs in written or spoken form; the other is the non-verbal modes, presented in other semiotic forms, such as pictures, music, films graphs and etc. The buttons in the elevators can the best exemplification of the marriage of different modes in communication. Pressing a button in the elevators can provide the passengers with information in both verbal and non-verbal modes simultaneously, numbers on the controlling panel, a voice message from the loudspeaker, different colors of lights around the buttons and a system of the tactile mode known as Braille, a non-linguistic system design for the blind in which a system of raised dots that can be read with the fingers by people who are blind or who have low vision. It is imperative to demonstrate how the mixing modes occurring simultaneously convey information to the receivers and measure the communicative effectiveness upon them. Communication in its forms can be regarded as the results of the mixing modes which may be perceived in a mono-modal or multi-modal sense by the receivers.

Therefore, multimodal discourse analysis is an approach to discourse that focuses on how meaning is made through the use of multiple modes of communication as opposed to just language in discourse analysis. As a matter of fact, the study of multimodal modes can be regarded as a recurrence of semiotic study. As an interdisciplinary study, it will propel the development of both semiotics and linguistics.

Similar to lexical choices in linguistic communication, those semiotic choices of both verbal and visual modes as social practices are also context-

Chapter II Review of Related Literature

based and function-oriented in social and political activities. In addition, because of the above-mentioned presuppositions of the unbalanced distribution and dominance of power and the manipulation of ideology in social interaction concerned by the critical linguists, any semiotic products, such as pictures, colors, sounds, sculptures, gestures, and the like may indicate kinds of the implied meaning of stances, identities, views, values and activities, which must be profitable to those who are in the dominant position but cognitively or behaviorally misguiding to others who are dominated. MCDA, being the critical study of multi-modal communications, focuses on the multimodal communications referring to the process of meaning making in the underlying repertoire of choices, of meaning potentials. For example, even the seemingly naturalized choice of a lady's sweet and soft voice in the broadcasting system in the elevator can mirror the ubiquitous stereotype of women's pre-determined image and position in the workplace.

For discourses with political intentions, it is conceivable that an excellent multimodal design of discourse seems to be more essential for its manipulative force. The figure below is a screen capture with a transcript of an off-screen male voice coming from one piece of Donald Trump's televised presidential campaign advertising named *Two USs-Immigration* during his running for US presidency in 2016. It aims to make a comparison between two different future policies towards Syrian Refugees to be launched by Donald Trump and Hillary Clinton so as to persuade the voters to vote for him.

Figure 4 Off-screen Male Voice: Syrian Refugees Flood in

A brief look at the screen capture can communicate information to the voters more than they would expect. The televised advertising is commonly a mixture of both verbal and visual modes with background music. On the linguistic level, it can be easily figured out that the choice of the metaphorical word "flood" makes the propaganda vivid and pervasive; the concrete number "65,000" cited by his rival enhancing its objectivity; the affirmative sentences structures indicating a fact of crisis. On the level of non-linguistic level, people can see a large crowd of people gathering together, the image of which is metaphorically depicted in a vague and grey picture. Among the crowd are two persons in the front position: a man and a woman described as typical images of people from the Middle East countries, which can expose their identities—Syrian refugees. In addition, the bass background music sounds grave and gloomy.

  An investigation into the elements, such as, participants, behaviors, goals, values and locations in the advertising suggests that the cooperation of both linguistic and non-linguistic modes serve the same theme in Trump's advertising, that is, Hillary's loose immigration policy may be harmful and dangerous to the US via the creation of a concrete, pervasive, objective and striking effect. However, assuming that only linguistic or non-linguistic mode existed here, the communicative effect would be constrained. Without linguistic mode, the picture is not informative and precise enough with the loss of its effectiveness because words are more plausible to the audience, while without the assistance of non-linguistic mode, it is not effective enough with the loss of its efficiency because pictures are more perceptible to the observers. Therefore, several assumptions about the composition of different modes in televised political advertising can primarily be made from the perspective of MCDA, which will be elaborated in details in the following chapters:

  Firstly, the semiotic resources applied in the production of any televised political advertising should consist of both the verbal and non-verbal modes. The former refers to the linguistic system of communication in both oral and textual form such as monologue, dialogues, interviews, slogans, off-screen voices, screen texts and so on. The latter one, as non-linguistic system of communication, is composed of the visual modes including color saturation,

Chapter Ⅱ Review of Related Literature

framing, shape, body movement, the focus of the lens, etc, and the vocal modes including background music, timbre, and sound effect and the like. The combination of these two semiotic resources, functioning as semiotic choices in meaning-making, should be taken into consideration in multimodal discourse analysis simultaneously.

Secondly, it can be safely assumed that the more modes the advertising employs, the more informative it will be, as any change of the symbolic expressions can generate new meaning. However, it doesn't mean that any addition or subtraction of different modes in televised political advertising can be treated as a simple calculation of meaning-making that can strengthen the communicative force. In other words, those semiotic resources are not organized randomly but artistically and artificially. Modes with their respective characteristics, known as multimodal complexity, should be arranged in an appropriate way (Boeriis, 2008). Generally speaking, the verbal modes are still the dominant parts in political discourse for its primary requirement on authenticity, objectivity and exactness of the information. The non-verbal modes are necessary counterparts which play decisive roles in the substitution, illustration, extension, salience, empathy and rhetoric of the information transmitted by linguistic forms. All in all, the tactic semiotic choices and collaborations in political adverting aim to maximize its communicative potential by the realization of "meaning potential" in the process of meaning-making in certain contexts.

Thirdly, being consistent with the ideas and values of the dominant group, the multimodal designs in the televised political advertising, as another kind of social practice, should fundamentally contribute to the realization of the their social, cultural, and political interests. In terms of the distribution of power in society, its impurity determines the situation that not every one has the equal opportunity to have access to the social resources. Let's take the mass media for example. For better manipulation of the thought, those semiotic resources in mass media, for instance, television, newspapers, magazines. etc. , can be deliberately and arbitrarily abused to generate meanings that are naturalized in form, but ideological in content.

Therefore, the study on those semiotic modes in the political advertising must be encoded and decoded in an ideological way, displaying a certain kind of power relation in social practice. Apart from the explicit meaning on the surface, the strong "political intentions" buried in them should be studied and identified in a critical way.

Chapter III

Televised Political Advertising

3.1 Political Advertising

As Lakoff (1990) holds that politics is language, in turn, language is politics, the relationship between them is internal and indispensable. Narrowly speaking, the combination of language and politics is known as political discourse, which, according to Chilton and Schaffner (2011), emphasizes the role of language in politics. However, as it has been proven previously that discourse can be signified through both verbal and non-verbal semiotic choices, political discourse can be regarded as a certain genre of verbal or non-verbal communication conducted by political participants for any political intention as well. In other words, the characteristics of political discourse should be associated with political actors, political process and political context. Any form of political communication, such as political advertising, political pamphlets, parliament speech, the State of Union Address, presidential debates and, etc. are the primary and reliable data resources of political discourse analysis (PDA).

Generally speaking, advertising is a means of communication with the users of a product or service. Advertisements are messages paid for by those who send them and are intended to inform or influence people who receive them, as defined by the Advertising Association of the UK. Though all advertising shares the same ways of transmission, that is, communications in written forms, such as pamphlets, circulars, fliers, billboards, bumper stickers, or communications broadcasted by radio or television, the primary distinction of political advertising from other forms of advertising mainly depends on its two themes as follows:

> Political advertising includes communications supporting or opposing a candidate for nomination or election to either a public office or an office of a political party (including county and precinct chairs).
> Political advertising includes communications supporting or opposing an officeholder, a political party, or a measure (a ballot proposition).

Therefore, it can be seen that political advertising, also known as campaign advertising, refers to a kind of verbal or visual communication produced or paid by politicians or political parties for the purpose of winning over the support of the public in a political campaign. In this sense, not a concrete product but political stances or politicians themselves have been the main participants in the advertising.

It should come as no surprise that a great effort of attention to its effectiveness, functions, contents and language use has been lavished in televised political advertising (Louden, 1989; Kaid, Nimmo, & Sanders, 1986). Some studies conducted on its effects in presidential campaign reveal that the successful design of televised political advertising is one of the important factors in influencing the potential voters (Basil, Schooler, & Reeves, 1991; Cundy, 1986; Garramone, 1985; Garramone, Atkin, Pinkleton, & Cole, 1990; Garramone & Smith, 1984; Hill, 1989; Just, Crigler, & Wallach, 1990; Kaid, 1991; Kaid, 1997; Kaid, Leland, & Whitney, 1992; Kaid & Sanders, 1978; Lang, 1991; Meadow & Sigelman, 1982; Newhagen & Reeves, 1991; and Thorson, Christ, & Caywood, 1991). Statistics originated from the experimental research suggest that televised political advertising is proved to be more efficient than the traditional way of news report in the spread of information (Brians & Wattenberg, 1996; Kern, 1989; Patterson & McClure, 1976). The United

Chapter Ⅲ Televised Political Advertising

States holding its "leading" position in the construction and maintenance of the capitalist political system, there have also been a number of studies that compare televised political advertising in the United States with advertising from other countries (Foote, 1991; Griffin & Kagan, 1996; Holtz-Bacha & Kaid, 1995; Holtz-Bacha, Kaid, & Johnston, 1994; A. Johnston, 1991; Kaid, 1991; or Kaid & Holtz-Bacha, 1995a, 1995b). A few studies discuss agenda-setting and political advertising (Ghorpade, 1986; Roberts & McCombs, 1994; Schleuder, McCombs, & Wanta, 1991). Several studies adopt more of a rhetorically oriented approach to political advertising (Cronkhite, Liska, Schrader, 1991; Descutner, Burnier, Mickunas, & Letteri, 1991; Gronbeck, 1992; Jamieson, 1989; Larson, 1982; Shyles, 1991; Smith & Johnston, 1991; Kaid & Johnson, 2001). Based on the Corpus-based analysis of the televised presidential advertising from the year of 1952 to 1996, Benoit (1999) proposed a function-based research method to televised political advertising, categorizing the themes in advertising into "acclaims (self-praise or positive remarks), attacks (negative remarks) and defenses (self-justification)" so as to explore their influence on the public in the enactment of political power. Later, Benoit (2003) extends his functional theory to a larger-scale analysis of various political campaign discourses in the election year of 2000, such as primary and general campaign advertising, political debates, radio advertising, talk show and the like. Recently, the study of political advertising has become a purely linguistic study. Ndimele (2015) talks about language use, especially word choices in political advertising and chooses the qualitative aspect of content analysis that was used from a rhetorical perspective, as the discourse approach for evaluating "See who wants to be President of Nigeria", presented in the political commercial on television.

3.2　American General Election Campaign Advertising

It is widely believed that one of the outstanding features in so-called US political system lies in its possibilities in the selection and retention of the peoples' choices for president and allowance for the public to express its policy preferences. US presidential election is a quadrennial competition mainly between the two political parties, the Democratic Party and the Republic Party, and their respective nominees for the highest position in the nation. The complex procedures of US presidential election can be roughly divided into two phases: the Primary Period and the General Period.

The first phase usually starts from the beginning of the election year and ends at the mid-year. The form of a primary is universal suffrage, a state of the two parties (the Democratic Party and the Republican Party) voters to the polls to vote "pledged delegates" who would attend the National Convention of the Party, and express support for a candidate of this Party. Then, the two parties will always hold the National Convention of the Party respectively to determine the final presidential candidate and vice presidential candidate of the Party and discuss the presidential campaign platform in July or August.

The declaration of the nomination of the candidates by the two Parties marks the end of the first phase and the beginning of the second phase, which includes a series of general election campaign activities, popular vote and inauguration. The general election campaign usually begins at the end of August, lasting eight or nine weeks. During this time, the presidential candidates of both parties will spend large amounts of money in all parts of the country with massive advertising campaign, and they will also hold some campaign speeches, meet voters, press conferences, as well as public debates. In order to gain the voters' confidence to win more votes, candidates will elaborate on the policy in favor of domestic and international affairs on

Chapter III Televised Political Advertising

different occasions. National voters elect on the following day of the first Monday of November of that year, known as the presidential election date. All US voters head to the designated locations for voting and make a choice between the two presidential candidates (with a ballot to elect the state's presidential "electoral"). After the presidential inauguration, the United States presidential election will end.

During the two phases in the election, the primary one and the general one, the latter is considered to be more attractive and significant just for two reasons. Firstly, it is not only the direct face-to-face competition for the presidency between the two candidates but also the power struggle between the two political parties. More significantly, for the majority of the population, most of them keep their distance from politics; it is not until the declaration of the presidential candidates that a series of campaign activities can call their attention to the advent of the election year. The campaign is a great spectacle. Some excitement may be generated and some diversion (as well as annoyance) provided for those who turn on the television to find that their favorite program has been preempted by political talk or who answer the telephone only to hear a prerecorded message exhorting them to vote (Nelson, Steven & David, 2012). Conversation about politics increases and some citizens become intensely involved as they get caught up by campaign advertising and mobilization (Nelson, Steven & David, 2012).

Therefore, the candidates' performance in the general election campaign activities will directly influence the ultimate result in the electoral vote and the ownership of presidency. Though, this is particularly true in campaigns at the national level, where voters have little personal contact with presidential candidates and must rely on experiencing candidates through political contexts via mass media. Before the television age, there was a time in US politics when it was seen as uncouth for presidential candidates (especially incumbents) to campaign. They might make some public addresses at campaign rallies, but for the most part, they left the campaigning to the political parties and their staffs (CNN all Politics). The evolution of television has offered US public an even more seemingly authentic and intimate view of presidential candidates, transmitting every step of the respective campaign trails. In the programs, like televised campaign spots, presidential debates, talk show, those candidates spare no in the interpretation of their future administrative policies, the shaping of their personal imagines and characteristics, the attacking and defaming of their rivals and the self-defense of their own weaknesses. As a result of too much emphasis on television, especially on televised advertising, Gurevitch and Blumler (1990) assert that US style politics has become the model for other democracies. Because of the need of more direct control over the style and image conveyed to voters, televised political advertising provides a unique opportunity for the candidate to control this interaction with the voters and to control the way he or she is presented (Kaid, 1981).

There are two kinds of political advertising in the US: paid and free ones. Though a large amount of money should be poured into the paid advertising, it is reported that television advertising is by far the most expensive item in a campaign's budget (Hornick, 2011). West (1997) also observed that "television advertising is the single biggest expenditure in most major campaigns today". Statistics on the increasing costs during the election indicate that it is more preferable for the politicians to choose the paid advertising, on the one hand, just because of no limits in the choice, modification and design of the topic, contents, styles, and ways of presentation in the paid advertising (Kaid & Holtz-Bacha, 2006), and on the hand, fundraising is a signal of its strength, for the bombast of television advertising also allows campaigns to get ahead in the media wars—on TV, radio, online, in the mail—and on-the-ground grassroots outreach. Here are the amounts spent on all federal elections, by cycle. The following two figures provided by Political Action Commission (PAC) illustrate the total amount of money spent by the two parties and their respective candidates in the congressional races, trying to influence federal elections in the congressional races and in the presidential election cycle from 2000 to 2016.

Chapter Ⅲ Televised Political Advertising

Table 2 Total Amount of Money Spent on the Two Phases of the Election

The Presidential Cycle	Total Cost of Election	Congressional Races	Presidential Races	Congressional Races (%)	Presidential Races (%)
2016	$6,444,253,265	$4,057,519,568	$2,386,733,696	62.96%	37.04%
2012	$6,285,557,223	$3,664,141,430	$2,621,415,792	58.29%	41.71%
2008	$5,285,680,883	$2,485,952,737	$2,799,728,146	47.03%	52.97%
2004	$4,147,304,003	$2,237,073,141	$1,910,230,862	53.94%	46.06%
2000	$3,082,340,937	$1,669,224,553	$1,413,116,384	54.15%	45.85%

Table 3 Ratios of Total Amount of Money by the Two Parties in the US

The Presidential Cycle	Total Cost of Election	By Dems	By Repubs	Dem %	Repub %
2016	$6444253265	$3076968576	* $3078629166	0.48	0.48
2012	$6285557223	* $2786555430	$3245847596	0.44	0.52
2008	$5285680883	* $3006088428	$2239412570	0.57	0.42
2004	$4147304003	$2146861774	* $1963417015	0.52	0.47
2000	$3082340937	$1311910043	* $1662298674	0.43	0.54

* The Winner in the Election

As shown in Table 3, the amount of money spent on the election by the two parties and their own candidates shows a steady increase in the 21st Century from 2000 to 2016. In addition, though the expenditure spent on the congressional races is a little larger than that spent on the general except on the election year of 2008, it should be noted that the second phase is a face-to-face competition between two rivals and their respective parties and only lasts about two months from the end of August to the beginning of November with more than half of the money spent on campaign activities. Kaid (1996) claims that from national to state and local elections, 50 to 75 percent of a campaign's funds are typically spent on ad production and air time. Consequently, successful participation, especially in federal elections, requires large amounts of money, especially for television advertising.

Based on the analysis, several reasons can justify the selection of televised US General Election Campaign Advertising as the case study of political advertising:

First and foremost, America being an acknowledged superpower in the world, its mature and stable political system, in particular, the complete and open electoral system, is regarded as the best instantiation of political democratization, attracting most of the attention in academics. Realizing the significant role of televised political advertising in the US presidential election, too many researches are conducted on it from different perspectives. The results lay necessary research foundation for the current study. Thus, persuasion, reliability and practicality in the study can be assured.

Secondly, Bipartisan System in the US only involves two presidential candidates nominated by two main parties in the general election period; its dichotomous division is convenient for data collection, data classification and corpus analysis for the sake of its functions, that is, acclaiming, attacking and self-defense. Naturally, scientificity of the study can be guaranteed.

Thirdly, America is the first and model country to use television in presidential election. Its long history and rich experience in the creation, transmission, management and innovation of televised political advertising system can be another crucial fact in the study.

Finally, enough funds is a prerequisite for the application of the most advanced modern technology in multimedia-making design and transmission, such as, Full HD Video, computer-generated imagery (CDI), animation technology and speech synthesis, which can facilitate the comprehensive analysis of all the multimodal semiotic resources.

Chapter IV

Theoretical Framework

The present study offers a comprehensive analysis of both verbal and visual modes in televised political advising. The classification of the corpus collected should be under the guidance of Benoit's functional approach to political discourse. The theoretical framework for the analysis of verbal modes is anchored on the systemic-functional grammar and its three meta-functions: ideational function, interpersonal function and textual function. The interpretation of VG, developed from the systemic-functional grammar, paves the way to study the visual modes. At last, we should posit the theoretical framework of the present research through the comprehensive study of verbal-visual interaction, with its focus on the study upon multimodal political discourses from a critical perspective.

4.1 Benoit's Functional Approach to Political Discourse

Through diachronic analysis of large-scale corpora gathering from campaign activities from 1956 to 2000, Benoit (2000, 2004) proposes a functional technique to Political Campaign Discourse. Benoit (2004) considers "voting as a comparative act". In other words, one candidate should distinguish himself from his rivals in future policy and personal characters. Therefore, the purpose of any campaign activity aims to establish voters' preferability and admiration to the candidates themselves meanwhile to arouse voters' distrust and dissatisfaction with their rivals. Generally speaking, candidates have three options in televised political advertising according to Benoit:

 They can acclaim (engage in self-praise of one's positive accomplishments or qualities),

 They can attack (criticize other candidates for failures or negative qualities), and

 They can defend (refute attacks).

As a matter of fact, such a kind of classification conforms to the interactional and socio-cognitive strategy that people tend to make positive self-presentation and negative other-presentation or at least to avoid a negative impression in face-to-face competition. Therefore, all the verbal and non-verbal corpora can be functionally classified into two categories, namely, acclaim and attack on the basis of participants involved in the discourse.

4.2 Systemic-functional Grammar

Systemic-functional grammar (SFG) is a system to linguistic description for the purpose of providing a comprehensive account of how language is constructed and used in context of communication. Literally, the name of SFG indicates that the study should be composed of two different but closely related grammars: one is systemic grammar and the other is functional grammar. For one thing, Halliday, partly influenced by the theory of formalism initiated by Saussure, focuses on the systemic study of the morphological and syntactic features in a well-formed structure in traditional sense. More significantly, it occurs to him that the limited number of grammatical rules and lexicons can produce the unlimited number of meanings (meaning potential), the functional view that all languages in meaning-making should be a kind of grammatical and lexical choices serving

Chapter IV Theoretical Framework

for the realization of threemetafunctions, namely, ideational, interpersonal and textual functions should be adopted. Lemke (1998) points out that Halliday's functional classification for language provides a useful framework for understanding the interaction of multiple semiotic modalities in traditional and new multimedia and that metafunctions characterize aspects of meaning-making that apply to all semiotic resources. Thus, the theoretical foundation on the verbal modes in the present research should be based on his theory. The meanings realized through the lexicogrammar are different in nature and therefore belong to different categories. It can thus be identified that the ideational function, a functional component of how our experience of language and other semiotic systems are construed scientifically as meaning; the interpersonal function, one that has to do with the speaker's attitude and the interaction between the participants of the communication; and the textual function, one that has to do with the organization of the two other functions in terms of cohesion.

4.2.1 Ideational Function

Ideational meta-function can be subdivided into experiential function and logical function, which serve for the expression of "content": that is, of the speaker's experience of the real world, including the inner world of his own consciousness. Such a function in language system is mostly realized by transitivity, referring to the relationship between the verb and its dependent elements of structure. In order to express our experience, language users have to choose various processes or known as "going-on" which is composed of happening, doing, sensing, meaning, being and becoming. According to Halliday (1985), the transitivity system construes the world of experience into a manageable set of process type. It consists of six types: material process, mental process, relational process, behavioral process, existential process and verbal process. At the same time, it presents the participants and all the circumstantial elements associated with each process as Table 4 illustrates.

Table 4 Typical Functions of Group and Phrase Classes

Type of element	typically realized by
process	verbal group
participation	nominal group
circumstance	adverbial group or prepositional phrase

Grammatically speaking, the three concepts, as three semantic categories, are represented by linguistic structures referring to actual experience. The realization of a clause in its ideational function involves the selection of process types and transitivity functions which realize the process, participants and circumstances typically structured as verbal group, nominal group and prepositional group respectively as it is illustrated in the following example:

Table 5 Linguistic Structures

Participation	Process	Participation	Circumstance	Circumstance
The soldiers	kicked	the door	crazily	with a hammer.

Material processes, known as the process of doing, refer to the representation of outer experience. In Halliday's words, it means that this process expresses the notion that some entity "does" something—which may be done to some other entity (ibid). Concrete actions and a possible consequence or result can be depicted in the material process in which the actor, being the logical subject, means the participants of the action comparable to theme or subject, while the goal means the target of the action. Apart from the concrete action expressed in the material process, the abstract or metaphorical action or event can also be expressed in the material process.

Mental processes are related to the processes of sensing, such as feeling, thinking and seeing which are marked with those verbs showing the conscious activities of human beings. The structure of a mental process is composed of *senser* and *phenomenon* which are comparable to the two participants of actor and goal in the material process with a verb inserted between them in SFG, the senser is the conscious being that is feeling, thinking or seeing, the phenomenon is that which is sensed (Halliday,

Chapter IV Theoretical Framework

1985) and the verb can be sub-divided into three categories: perception (seeing, hearing, etc.), affection (liking, fearing, etc.) and cognition (thinking, knowing, and understanding, etc.).

Relational processes, also known as processes of being, is the third main type of processes appearing in discourses (Halliday, 1985). There are three kinds of sub-types in relational process, namely, intensive, circumstantial and possessive processes. In the intensive process the two nominal groups are linked by the typical word "be" or the other verbs functioning as "be" in terms of grammar, such as, *become, turn, remain, stay, seem, appear, end up, turn out, look, sound, smell, feel, taste*, etc. In the possessive process, the relationship between two nominal groups is one of ownership with the words *have, own, contain, include, involve, comprise* or *belong to* connecting them.

Verbal processes represent the processes of saying through the indicative verb which means "to say" in the form of direct speech or indirect speech. There are three elements in a verbal process: sayer, receiver and verbiage (Halliday, 1994). The sayer can be a human, a human-like speaker or an inanimate item; the receiver refers to the person to whom the saying is directed; the verbiage can be the nominalised content of what is said or the name of what is said.

Halliday distinguishes the direct speech from indirect speech; the former one refers to the clause directly quoted as in the first example (She explained "I am sick".), while the latter refers to the clause indirectly reported as in the second example (She explained she was sick.). For example:

Table 6 Direet Speech and Indiret Speech

She	explained	"I am sick".
Sayer	Process	Quoted
Quoting		

She	explained	she was sick.
Sayer	Process	Reporting
Reporting		

The differentiation made by Halliday is significant in terms of its function. As the figure indicates that there are two processes in each clause: the verbal clause and the relational process. Though the verbal clauses are the exactly the same, the relational processes in the examples are different. The selection between the direct speech and indirect speech given by different participants may generate various implications. In terms of critical study on the texts, the participant in the verbal process may be closely related with power relationship.

Behavioral processes refer to those of physical and psychological behavior, like breathing, coughing, smiling, dreaming and starring. Structurally, behavioral clauses always involve a Behaver, which is realized by a nominal group denoting a conscious being, like the Senser of a "mental" clause, and they are almost always middle, with the most typical pattern being Behaver and Process.

Existential processes refer to clauses with the verbs "to be" or synonyms such as "exist" "arise" or occur", which can inform the hearers that something exists or happens. For example, there is a negotiation. In the invented sentences, the participant, preceded by *there be* or there exist, may be any kind of phenomenon and often denote a nominalised action.

Thompson (1996) comments that we need to set up categories detailed enough to make us feel that we have captured something important about the meaning, but broad enough to be manageable as the basis for general claims about the grammar of English. In fact, all these six kinds of processes can be sorted out in the grammar of the clause rather than verbs. The transformation among those processes with the help of such strategies as voice transformation, nominalization and lexical choices may deliver different meanings to the audience by indicating, modifying or concealing the participation adaptively. As a kind of meaning potential in meaning-making, such a transformation underlying the speaker's different ideas, values, attitudes and positions naturally reflects the speaker's communicative intentions which should be denaturalized in certain social contexts. Therefore, what kind of these six processes that the speaker tends to choose may largely be determined by the ideology he/she holds or his/her social status. As the same event can be treated to be different processes, meanings can be expressed quite differently. Therefore, the analysis upon transitivity can expose the buried relationship among power, language and ideology, which should be adopted to be an important analytic tool in CDA.

4.2.2 Interpersonal Function

Emphasizing the necessity of interaction between the speaker and the audience, Bakhtin (1984) firstly proposed the concept of interpersonal meaning in 1929. Bakhtin stated that people interacted with each other in communicative activities; they either provided or asked information.

As Halliday (2003) proposes that language not only construes experience, but simultaneously acts out "the interpersonal encounters that are essential to our survival". In other words, apart from the ideational function, another metafunctions of language refers to the interpersonal function which serves to establish and maintain social relations between speakers and addressee, to express the speaker's viewpoint on events and things in the world, and to influence the addressee's behavior or views through the grammatical choices in linguistic system. This includes the various ways the speaker enters a speech situation and performs a speech act. Several grammatical systems, such as mood system, modality system, personal pronouns, quotations, play fundamental roles in completing interpersonal function in grammar.

Mood structures express interactional meaning "what the clause is about, as a verbal exchange between speaker-writer and audience" (Halliday, 1994). It consists of two parts: one is the subject, which is a nominal group and the other is the finite operator, which is part of a verbal group. Subjects refer to nouns or any counterparts of nouns such as word, phrases or even clauses; the finite operator refers to the traditional auxiliaries like *does*, *did*, *is*, *was*, *has*, *had*, *will*, *shall*, *can*, *may* and *must*. In addition to the mood, there remains an extra part known as residue which includes predicator, complement and adjunct. For example, the following diagram can illustrate the distribution of elements in the mood structure of a clause and its residue part:

Table 7 The Mood Structure of a Clause and Its Residue Part

My brother	has	already	donated	all his money	to the poor.
Subject	Finite	Adjunct	Predicator	Complement	Complement
Mood		Residue			

The utilization of mood systems includes two primary grammatical categories of the indicative (with further subtypes of the declarative and the interrogative), which is characteristically used to exchange information, and also the imperative, which is used to exchange goods-and-services. The presence of subject followed by finite (My brother plus will) indicates that it is an indicative clause as the example shows clearly, while the absence of them an imperative clause. Meanwhile, the order of subject and infinite determine the mood of the clauses. The order subject before finite realizes declarative sentences, while the order finite before subject realizes interrogative sentences.

Modality system is another major component in realizing the degrees or scales of the interpersonal relationship in communication. The introduction of modality into SFG results from the limits of the finite element which is inherently either positive or negative as Halliday (1985) claims that the possibilities are not limited to a choice between yes or no; there exists some intermediate degrees between them known as modality. In other words, the selections in the degree of modality mirror the speaker's subtle changes of attitude, such as determination, offer, proposal, command, proposition, obligation, reprimand. etc, resulting from the differentiation in their social relationship and communicative intentions. The subtle variation in modality lies in either lexical or grammatical choice. Lexical expressions include adverbs indicating possibilities such as "possibly" "maybe" "probably" "presumably" "supposedly", for example. Grammatical expressions refer to the modal verbs, indicating mastery, responsibility or possibility such as "can" "may" "must" "shall" "will". According to Halliday and Matthiessen (2004), "modality also involves degrees and scales, and it is classified into

Chapter IV Theoretical Framework

high, median and low value".

The study upon discourses aims to probe into the commitment that the speaker makes in his discourse and to figure out the attitude of the speaker towards the interaction and the relationship with his hearer from the perspective of interpersonal function. Further, it will disclose the social distance between the participants of the communication (speaker and hearer) and the relationship between power and control. Thus, it is apparent that modality becomes one of the most reliable and effective analytical standards in CDA.

Personal pronoun has the characteristic of "anaphoric reference", as Brown & Gilman (1972) suggests that the selection of a certain personal pronoun in many languages will be affected by the social status, power and intimacy between the participants of the discourse. Similarly, Levinson (1983) insists that the encoding of personal pronoun shows "the social identities of participants or the social relationships between them, or between one of them and persons and entities referred to". Personal pronouns can be divided into two categories: inclusive and exclusive pronouns, the selections of which can indicate certain scales of power and solidarity. The following diagram shows the dimensions of solidarity and power with the transformation of pronouns.

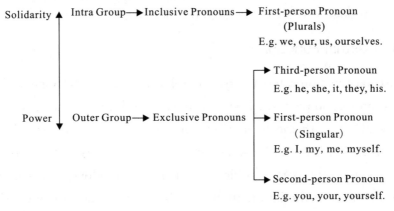

Figure 5 Dimension of Solidarity and Power with the Shift of Pronouns

It is clear that the inclusive pronouns referring to the first-person pronouns such as *we*, *us* and *our* can show great solidarity, indicating the support each other or for the intra group, especially in political or international affairs. Therefore, the repetitive use of inclusive Pronouns can assist the politicians in expressing great intimacy and shorten the social distance with the public. Comparatively, the use of exclusive pronouns shows the reduction of solidarity and the fortification of power. Therefore, as the core question in the study of interpersonal function is to probe into how the speaker constructs the social relationship with the audience in the discourse or texts, the representation of the identity of the participants should be explored.

Quotations, referring to direct speech and indirect speech, also involve the contrived construction of the social interactions, as Xin (2005) points out that in various discourses, especially, news reports, direct speech and indirect speech can make the speaker's presentation more persuasive and powerful by introducing the speeches of witnesses, actors, mass media or authority (government, officials or local personalities). Such effectiveness stems from the common belief that people tend to accept objective information from definite sources or those coming from higher social status or authority. Naturally, the speakers, in their discourses, frequently use direct or indirect speeches to make their hearers firmly believe what they say, even though it can't be testified on the spot.

4.2.3 Textual Function

Textual function refers to creating relevance to context. One of the most essential notions in the textual aspect is the theme-rheme structure. According to Halliday (1985), theme is the "starting-point for the message" or "the ground from which the clause is taking off". Rheme represents the remainder of the message, the part in which the theme is developed. In general, the content of theme is the information that the speakers aim to emphasize. For example,

Chapter Ⅳ　Theoretical Framework

Table 8　The Transformation of Theme-Rheme Structure

Tom	stands on the platform.
Subject	Predicate
Theme	Rheme

Stands on the platform	Tom
Subject	Predicate
Theme	Rheme

According to Table 8, Tom is obviously regarded to be the grammatical subject in both sentences, but the themes are quite different in these sentences due to different communicative goals. As Fairclough commented that it is always worth attending to what is pleased initially in clauses and sentences, because "that can give insight into assumptions and strategies which may at no point be made explicit" (Fairclough, 1992), it is quite natural for the speakers, especially, politicians, to start their speeches with various themes because of his power, stand and ideology they hold.

4.3　Visual Grammar

Adopting a social semiotic view towards language, Halliday's SFG with its focus on the semiotic system, treats discourses or texts as both grammatical and lexical choices in meaning-making to achieve three metafunctions. Therefore, the selection of visual resources as another representation of meaning potential, two prerequisites for the creation of visual grammar could be satisfied. Firstly, the focus on the semantic system of language makes it possible to extend its theory to the study of visual modes in meaning-making, expression and interpretation, as any kind of social interaction both in verbal and visual forms can be regarded as the process of realizing meaning potential, the mechanism of which is the same as lexico-grammar in language, that is, the inventory and application of elements and rules underlying socio-specific and cultural-specific forms of verbal and visual communication. Secondly, linguistic forms are regarded as part of social semiotics, its emphasis on the roles any symbolic sign plays in the operation of social practices also encourages a functional view towards the study of visual modes. Therefore, under the influence of Halliday's theory, Kress and Van Leeuwen (1996, 2006), firstly set up a framework of visual grammar in their book *Reading Images: The Grammar of Visual Design*, which is commented as the systematic and exhaustive elaboration of how the visual images construct meanings in social interaction. Machin (2013) comments that their groundbreaking publication marks the integration between multimodality and linguistics. Kress and Van Leeuwen (2006) apply the metafunctions in SFG to visual modality, and identify the purpose of this text so as to define a theoretical and descriptive framework that can be used for visual analysis. Kress and Van Leeuwen (2006) note that "not all the relations that can be realized linguistically can also be realized visually or vice versa", the similar classification but different terminologies is adopted in the visual grammar.

When the visual grammar discussed, it should be initially understood that grammar in this sense refers to the basic rules governing the construction and presentation of visual elements that are created for inclusion in a motion picture. These are the commonly accepted guidelines that define how visual information should be displayed to a viewer. According to VG the meaning of visual modes consists of three kinds, namely, representational meaning, interactive meaning and compositional meaning, respectively correspondent to the threemetafunctions in functional grammar proposed by Halliday: ideational function, interpersonal function and textual function as indicated below.

Table 9 Corresponding Relations between SFG and VG

Systemic-functional Grammar	Visual Grammar
Ideational Function	Representation Meaning
Interpersonal Function	Interactive Meaning
Textual Function	Compositional Meaning

Chapter IV Theoretical Framework

4.3.1 Representational Meaning

Kress and Van Leeuwen (2006) propose that any semiotic system outside any system of signs can be on behalf of the experience of the world in a referential sense. Similar to the ideational function in the SFL, representational meaning is first of all conveyed by the abstract or concrete "participants" (people, places or things) depicted. Different from the classification of six processes in the functional grammar, only two interrelated processes are recognized in the visual grammar. One is narrative process indicating the on-going actions and events, easily changes in process and momentary spatial arrangement. The other is the conceptual representations presenting actions and events that are more stable, free from the boundary of time and more general in nature.

Narrative Representations

As indicated by its name, the action process involves an action or movement. The actor of the action usually conducts a vector or the action itself is a vector which can be human or non-human. And compared with the background, the fore grounded actor and action tend to be more salient. The actor is the participant who initiates the vector. When there are two participants in the action process, one is actor, and the other is goal. The goal is the participant who receives the vector, so it is also called the object of the action. In accordance with the fact of whether there is a goal or not, the process can be further divided into two types: transactional and non-transactional processes. The following comparison of three screenshots helps to illustrate their differentiation:

Jackie Chan shot the man   Jackie Chan shot

Figure 6 Comparison between Transactional and Non-transactional Processes

Apparently, both of the two pictures have foregrounded actors with guns in hand and trying to shoot. The vector belongs to the same process of the action of shooting. However, the first picture has a definite goal—a man in blue; while in the latter the goal is not definite in the picture, instead, this is the interaction between the goal and the audience. As the two pictures belong to transactional process and non-transactional process respectively, the impression upon their viewers is different. For the former one, the process is more authentic, objective and pervasive, while for the latter one, the process is less objective but more imaginative, emotional and impressive to the viewers. For its emphasis on the concrete actions made by the actor, it can be assumed that the transactional process should account for most of the actions in a televised political advertising as the main purpose of the advertising design aims to make a favorable or unfavorable portrait to the presidential candidates.

It should be noted that non-transactional process doesn't include any goal. Nor is its action formed by the actor. For example, the following is another picture of non-transactional process. It is symbolic, indicating the action of raining. Therefore, analogous to the intransitive verb in language, the non-transactional processes can be abstract and metaphorical.

A picture being a non-transactional process, its vagueness and inaccuracy in meaning-making can't express the real communicative purpose of the designer; its nonrepresentational features may be revealed but the concrete denotation may be concealed, which can mislead the viewers if no further complement or explanation is given.

Figure 7 Symbolic Indication of Raining

In reaction process, the vector is constructed only by the eye line, the direction of the gazes made by one or more of the represented participants. The actor and the goal in action process are respectively changed into reactor and phenomena. The reactor is the participant who does the looking and the

Chapter IV Theoretical Framework

phenomena is the participant which is being looking at. Similar to action process, the representational meaning in the reaction process can reveal the reactor's affection, perception and cognition. With the appearance of phenomena or not, it can also be further divided into two kinds, namely, transactional and non-transactional process up to whether there are the phenomena or not (Kress &. Van Leeuwen, 2006).

The two basic factors in reaction process should be illustrated: one refers to who or what the reactor looks at; the other refers to the directions of the gaze the reactors have projected. To recognize the two factors is crucial, as Machin and Mayr (2012) suggest that all these can be resources for guiding the viewer as to how they should evaluate the reactors' real purpose, even if this is not explicated stated. For example, the following several screenshots coming from a piece of public service advertising named *Can the Abortion Pill Be Reversed?* in the *New York Times* can help to give a detailed illustration on various semiotic choices and their composition in reaction processes.

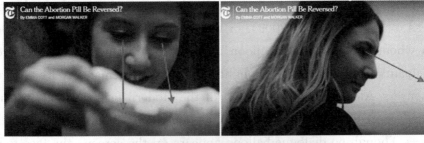

Figure 8 Can the Abortion Pill Be Reversed?

As the red arrows (the author notes) indicate in the picture, the young girl is looking at a baby's skirt without disctractions. Both the reactor and the phenomena appear in the picture, it is a transactional process which definitely tells us the truth that she wants to be a mother.

However, the second picture in Figure 8 shows that the young girl is looking downwards without definite phenomenon. Thus, it is non-transactional reaction process. The directions of her thoughtful and melancholy gaze can uncover her inner mind and attitudes towards the mental and psychological damages the Abortion Pill has brought to her.

The third picture is also non-transactional as there is an old lady but no phenomenon in the picture. Instead, the reactor can look into the viewers' eyes directly.

Verbal and mental process, equivalent to projective process in linguistic system, must be processes of mixing both linguistic forms and visual forms. Therefore, the terms in verbal and mental processes are borrowed from the SFG directly. A special vector appears in TV advertising, cartoons, comic strips, quotes in school textbooks, on the screens of automatic bank tellers, etc. "The oblique protrusions of the thought balloons and dialogue balloons that connect drawings of speakers or thinkers to their speech or thought" (Kress & Van Leeuwen, 2006). In verbal, participants in a verbal process from whom the "dialogue balloon" emanates are known as the sayers; participants from whom the "thought bubble" vector emanates are known as the sensers. Along with development of the modern technology, especially, the wide spread use of the multimedia tech help to innovate the verbal process. Though no dialogue balloon appears on the screen, the face-to-face interviews, public speech, talk shows and etc launched by the Sayers which are broadcasted on TV or on the Internet can also be regarded as verbal processes, words in which can be transformed into texts. To some extent, the mechanism of the verbal process in visual grammar is quite similar to the direct speech in SFG. Therefore, it should be stressed that the words in the dialogue balloon, in the thought bubble or the transcript from the sound system should be recognized as other processes. As long as the Sayer speaks on the screen, his action of speaking can be treated as the verbal process. The following example is a short dialogue between a man and his girlfriend, which is a typical verbal process. The man declared "I love you", and then the girl replied "I know". Visually, two verbal processes can be identified, as there are two dialogue balloons. Verbally, the other two mental processes showing affection (I love you.) as well as perception (I know.) can be recognized under the guidance of the SFG.

Figure 9　Verbal Process

4.3.2　Conceptual Representations

The great difference between narrative and conceptual representations lies in the identifications of vectors in the image. For the former one, the vector is the necessary element while for the latter one, no vector exists. In other words, one is dynamic and concrete, denoting an action or behavior. On the contrary, the other, corresponding to existential and relational processes in linguistic forms, is comparatively abstract, static and symbolic so as to express the meaning of existence, possessions or sequence. According to Kress & Van Leeuwen (2006), the conceptual representation is comprised of three processes: classificational, analytical and symbolic processes.

In classificational processes, the related participants are classified in terms of a "kind of" relation, taxonomy: at least one set of participants will play the role of subordinates with respect to at least one other participant, the super-ordinate. Kress & Van Leeuwen (2006) distinguish convert taxonomy with overt taxonomy. In terms of convert taxonomy, the super-ordinate is implied while the subordinates of the same class are equally presented to the viewers in the same forms of the visual modes, such as size, color, distance to show the equality in sequence, power, ability, function, position and so on.

As soon as the super-ordinate appears in overt taxonomy, the ranks should be presented in the image, as the subordinate should be dominated by the super-ordinate. The categorization and domination can be demonstrated in visual forms such as diagrams, family trees or pictures with the selection of two directions: one is vertical or the other horizontal. In terms of the information value, the subordinate should be placed under or below the super-ordinate in the horizontal taxonomy, while the subordinate on the right of super-ordinate in vertical taxonomy.

Analytical processes are related to participants in terms of a part-whole structure. They involve two kinds of participants: one carrier (the whole) and any number of possessive attributes (the parts). In one analytical picture, there is no vector or tree structure (classificational process). "It serves to identify a carrier and to allow viewers to scrutinize this carrier's possessive attributes." (Kress and Van Leeuwen, 2006). From different perspectives, whether information arrangement in analytical processes organized orderly or not can be defined as structured or unstructured analytical processes respectively.

The analytical process appears commonly in political discourses, in the forms of different kinds of statistic graphs, procedures, deconstruction of objects, etc. Intergrating with language, it can provide viewers information of scientific, straight, precise, concrete and objective values.

Symbolic process focuses on what a participant means or is. It represents the participants as being representative of or standing for something else. Van Leeuwen and Kress (2006) divide symbolic processes into symbolic attributive and symbolic suggestive processes. Symbolic attributive process has more than one participant. The meaning or identity of the main participant or carrier is determined in relation to those of the other participants, functioning as attributes. One is the carrier whose identity has been established and the other participant represents meaning or identity. The symbolic suggestive process only involves one participant, the carrier

(Kress & Van Leeuwen, 1996), and its symbolic meaning is displayed by other elaborations.

4.3.3 Interactive Meaning

Apart from the function of representative meaning that visual resources are selected and integrated for the representation of interactions and the conceptual relations among various elements such as vectors, participants, sensers, phenomenon and circumstances in different processes depicted in images, their artificial and artistic arrangement aims to construct and maintain another kind of interaction, the interaction between the image makers and the viewers named as "interactive participants" (Kress & Van Leeuwen, 2006). That is to say, the producer's selection and integration of visual semiotic resources alike to linguistic choices made by speakers in interpersonal function can help to maintain the interaction between the represented participants and the viewers, establishing certain social relationships between them. In addition, the visual transmission of explicit and implicit meanings like the picture-maker's attitudes, ideas, values, ideology, stances, etc. can influence the viewers' physical and mental cognition towards the image as well as the real world around them. Generally speaking, the interactive meaning is realized by several factors: contact, size of frame, perspective and modality.

Contact

In terms of the contact system, absorbing Halliday's list of four basic functions that language can perform in the mood system, namely, to offer information, to offer service, to demand information and to demand goods and service, Kress and Van Leeuwen (2006) propose the alternative execution of two functions in images: "offer" and "demand". An image, being the production of the producers' mind, can be seen as another interface of referencing actual acts of interaction in talking. Its design determines the interaction between the producer and the viewers, generating different interactive meaning. Owing to the design in an image, the possible roles assigned to a viewer in such an interaction can be divided into two kinds: a passive observer or an active participant. Being passive observers, the viewers are not encouraged to be involved in the events described in the image. Instead, they are observers who are supplied with different information or service. Being active participant, the viewers are demanded to be engaged in the events and to make direct response to the participants, objects, circumstance, sharing with the producer's point of view, such as, request, order, appealing, approval, admiration, sympathy and the like, through eye contact along with facial expression, gestures, etc.

The choice of direct gazes is a primary and fundamental way to represent "demand image", while the avoidance of the gazes with the reactor is another way to represent "offer image". By means of direct eye contacts with the reactor in a non-transactional reaction process, the viewer has become the assumed phenomenon whom the reactor tries to look at. The reactor's continuous eye contacts with the viewers can help shorten the distance, making her words more stressful, persuasive and empathic. However, as it is indicated before, in the reaction process the reactors have to make two options: the option of phenomenon and the option of directions. Instead of direct eye contact with the viewers, they can choose to look upwards, downwards, leftwards and rightwards; they can simply close their eyes; they can look at any object in the image as the phenomenon or they can look off the frame aimlessly. All images that do not contain human or quasi-human participants looking directly at the viewer are of "offer image" in which no contact takes place. Obviously, the intentional choices made by the producer have become a meaning potential, revealing great implicit meaning. It should be noted that being strongly cultural-specific and contextual-specific, gazes may have different "metaphorical implications" (Machin, 2012). Its interpretation should be correlated to other kinds of body language and the existing circumstances.

The participants' facial expressions in the image can dissimulate psychological states towards their viewers and function as one of crucial factors in the establishment of social relationship between the producer and the viewers as well as for interaction between the participants and the viewers. As it is claimed that whether the "demand act" or "offer act" is largely determined by the eye lines, facial expressions should always accompany with different gazes. The great difference between gazes and facial expressions is that the former firstly constructs a certain relationship and then the latter can deliver the viewers kinds of attitudes and emotions concretely, which reversely contribute to the maintenance and consolidation of the relationship. As for the attitudes the facial expression possibly conveys, Ekman (2003) identifies seven universal facial expressions: anger, disgust, sadness, fear, surprise, contempt and happiness, which can be illustrated in the following pictures:

The Seven Universal Facial Expressions of Emotion

Figure 10   Seven Universal Facial Expressions of Emotion

Those facial expressions in the image belonging to the classification representations going with different gazes can generate various interactive meaning. For example, the lady having eye contact with the viewers can firstly attract their attention and shorten the distance with the audience; her smile show her intimacy, confidence and gratitude to get the viewer's approval and appreciation, which, in turn, results in the consolidation of the amicable relationship.

The choices of other gestures given by the participants can treated as another crucial factor determining the viewers' perception, interpretation and reception of kinds of attitudes, values and identities that the producer wants to express and kinds of social relationship that he wants to establish between the viewers and the represented participant in the image. For instance, pointing at another person with an extended finger is considered to be rude in many cultures.

Size of Frame

The judgment of spatial distribution among people and groups is another one of the most effective criteria in the judgment of their attitudes and social relations in social practice. It is noteworthy that space functions in communication are cultural-specific, and people from different cultural backgrounds may have different sense of space. Broadly speaking, however, scales of spatial distance zones can be recognized and roughly classified into three kinds: private, social and public, three of which can generate different interactive meanings. Private space is the most subjective and emotional, indicating intimate or personal relationship for the sake of expressing or seeking either positive attitudes like sympathy, trust, admiration, confidence, adoration, equality and protectionetc, or negative ones, such as terror, distrust, disgusting, hatred, attacking, fighting and so on. Social space can be used in impersonal and social gatherings. More formal, authentic, natural and neutral information can be expressed. The distance between two participants may be appropriate and comfortable for them to notice the most significant visual details. The public space is the most objective, with the loss of its focus on communication. Its use in public occasions can indicate vagueness, alienation and unfamiliarity.

In visual grammar, according to Kress and Van Leeuwen (2006), such interactive meanings transmitted from speakers to hearers can also be artificially contrived by the image producer through the shift of "size of frame", namely, the focus of a shot, technically, referring to the choice between close-up shot, medium shot and long shot, and so on. In the images, the close-up shot covers head and shoulders of the subject, the medium one approximately at the knees and the long shot showing the full figure. The close-up is the intimate shot, providing a magnified view of some person, object, or action. The medium shot is the shot type that nearly approximates how we, as humans, see the environment most immediately around us. The long shot is a more inclusive shot. It frames much more of the

Chapter IV Theoretical Framework

environment around the person, object, or action and often shows their relationships in physical space much better. There is no doubt that the choice of "size of frame" can contribute to the viewers' direct perception and attitude towards the image.

In a motive picture, the movement from close-up to long shot orvice versa depends on the photographer's concern on the creation of certain kinds of relationship between the image and its viewers as well as the relationship among the represented participants and objects depicted in it. Naturally, its spatial arrangement is strongly social and ideological, which can reflect different interactive meaning expressed by the spatial variation from private to public space mentioned before.

Perspective

Perspective is indicated by the angles of view, the third dimension of interactive meaning in image. The selections of angles or attitudes of how the image-makers consider the represented participants bring about the construction of relations between the represented participants and their viewers. Kress and Van Leeuwen (2006) distinguish "subjective images from objective images, meaning that the former ones with (central) perspective (and hence with a "built-in" point of view) and the latter ones without (central) perspective (and hence without a "built-in" point of view)".

The subjective images being a socialized, individual and unique products produced by the image-producer, whose inherent attitude or ideology could be imposed on the viewers. They are created through the perspective system. In other words, the subjective images make the viewer see what there is to see only from a particular point of view, consisting of two kinds of angles: horizontal angle and vertical angle.

The horizontal angle is related to the involvement or detachment between the image-producers and the represented participants (Kress and Van Leeuwen, 2006). Strong sense of involvement can be achieved by the choice of frontal angel, as if both the image-producers and the viewers, sharing the same points of view, should belong to certain groups of represented participants. On the contrary, the oblique angle can deliver a sense of detachment since it implies that the image-producers do not belong to any group of represented participants depicted in the image. Evidently, the choice of horizontal angle can imply the alignment and solidarity exixt among the image-producer and the represented participants in process of the image production. The following picture is aminiature of comic heads taken from all horizontal angles. From the first to the sixth picture, the involvement of the viewer decreases, while from the sixth to the eleventh picture, the detachment of the viewer decreases. Supposing that the represented participants stand still in a certain circumstance, the focus on its interaction with the circumstance, the image-producer and the viewers change along with the shift of the angle chosen by the image-producer.

As for the vertical angle, it "transmits power relationship between the represented participants and the viewers and between the represented participants within an image" (Guijarro & Sanz, 2008). There are three choices: high-angle, low-angle, and eye-level angle. In a high-angle picture, the represented participants are seen from a higher position while a low-angle picture is seen from below the represented participants. The choice of eye-level angle has little psychological effect on the viewer.

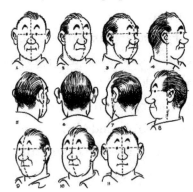

Figure 11　Classification of Sight Angle

Modality

The term "modality" stemming from linguistics refers to the truth value (positive or negative) or credibility and possibility of statements about the world. As it is demonstrated above, the system of modality focuses on such modality markers as the choices of modal verbs and adverbs which accord specific degrees of values to statements.

In visual grammar, modality means the degrees of reality, authenticity, reliability and certainty and truth of the message. Similar to the roles that the modal verbs play in the linguistic system, it can be realized by adapting

Chapter IV Theoretical Framework

various modality markers including color, contextualization, depth, illumination, and Brightness ranging from highest to lowest modality in visual grammar as well. Naturally, interactive meaning varies with the change of those modality markers. Machin and Mayr (2012) also insist on the significance of those modality makers, treating them as reliable instruments to figure out the meaning potential of the elements, features and styles of images in the critical study of all forms of visual communication.

However, it doesn't mean that the degree of modality increases with the enhancement of modality markers. The visual description of the sentence "Jim *need* drink a glass of pure water can't be a full colored or black-and-white one. As the actor, Jim should be colored while the goal, pure water, is colorless. It can happen in any place or an abstract setting. In terms of realism, the truth proposition should rely on its naturalistic features, that is to say, "on how much correspondence there is between what we can 'normally' see of an object, in a concrete and specific setting, and what we can see of it in a visual representation" (Kress and Van Leeuwen, 2006). Different from precise and unidirectional evaluation of modality in the use of modal verbs, therefore, the naturalistic modality enhances as articulation increases, but at a certain point it reaches its highest value and thereafter it decreases again.

Chrominance

Color or Chrominance in the age of modern technology plays a significant role as a marker of naturalistic modality that varies in various scales (Kress and Van Leeuwen, 2006):

> Degree of color saturation: a scale running from full color saturation to the absence of color; namely, to black and white.
> Degree of color differentiation: a scale running from a maximally diversified range of colors to monochrome.
> Degree of color modulation: a scale running from fully modulated color, with, for example, the use of many different shades of red, to plain, unmodulated color.

A comparison between linguistic and naturalistic modality scales could therefore be represented as in the following example:

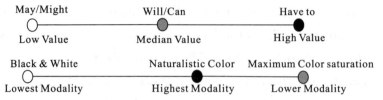

Figure 12　Variety of Modality in Modal Verbs and Color Saturation

As shown in Figure 12, it is more definite to define the values of modal verbs than to differentiate their values of different colors. Generally speaking, the modality reaches the highest when the choices of color conform to the reality. A naturalistic color picture, friendly and comfortable to one's eyes, can indicate great objectivity, reliability, certainty and authenticity. Naturalistic color can be regarded as a watershed; its change goes to two extremes. On one hand, the decrease of color in the aspects of saturation, differentiation and modulation leads to the increases of vagueness and uncertainty. A black and white picture has the lowest modality as it has lost most of the color details in the picture. Though simplicity can be expressed, comparatively negative attitudes, such as nostalgia, terror, uncertainty, monotony and the like reach to the utmost. The following two pictures come from two reports on the problem of fog and haze in Beijing.

Naturalistic color　　　　　　　　　　　　　Black and white

Figure 13　Exaggeration of Naturalistic Color

On the other hand, the exaggeration of naturalistic color results in intensified emotions for the purpose of emphasizing vivid, impressive and salient features. It often appears in cartoons, films and advertising, aiming

Chapter IV Theoretical Framework

to highlight certain characteristics of the represented participants. For example, the scarlet color is commonly used to emphasize the cruelty of a war. Apparently, its true value has been lowered, but the persuasive force may be fortified.

Contextualization refers to a scale running from the absence of background to the most fully articulated and detailed background. The naturalistic background reveals the highest modality, while the most fully articulated and detailed background, unfaithful to the reality, can produce more moderate modality than the absence of background with the lowest modality. Obviously, the degree of contextualization reflects how much spatial and chronological settings should be presented to the viewers. The shift from high to low contextualization can be regarded as a process from the concrete and narrative to the abstract as well as symbolic. In political advertising, the de-contextualized image mainly aims to reveal the distinctive identity of certain groups of people, such as, politicians, celebrities, terrorists, victims and etc. because from the public's point of view they should be the symbol of power, beauty, terror or suffering regardless of the change of settings. On the contrary, the contextualized image focuses on the description of real events, which can deliver certain kinds of truth, attitudes and emotions to the viewers.

Depth ranges from the absence of any depth to maximally deep perspective, with other possibilities between them. The deeper the perspective is, the higher the modality will be and vice versa. Therefore, the image-producer's decision on the amount of details exposed to the viewers lies in the possibilities of choosing certain scales of depth. In the maximally deep perspective, all the specifics in the image possibly perceived by the viewer indicates the highest modality, while the absence of any depth creats a vague picture to the views with the lowest degree of modality, expressing a sense of uncertainty and abstraction.

Illumination is another modality marker in the interactive meaning. It is concerned with the shade and light in the picture. It means the scale running from the fullest representation of light, which indicates higher degree of modality and shade, to the absence of the light and shade, indicating the lowest degree of modality. A naturalistic representation of light and shade can show the highest degree of modality. Therefore, the proper demonstration of shade and light determines the truth value of the picture.

Brightness also functions as a necessary indicator measuring the degree of modality. It refers to a scale running from a maximum number of different degrees of brightness to just two degrees: black and white or dark grey and light grey, or two brightness values of the same color. In physics, light coming from different directions may produce the corresponding shade. An image approaching the natural presentation of brightness has a higher level of modality, while the complete absence of light and shade marks the lowest level of modality.

In the US presidential election, the ultimate aim of any campaign activity is that candidates could obtain enough ballots from the voters to take over the presidency eventually. It is a process of struggle between candidates themselves meanwhile another process of solidarity among candidates and voters. It is safely assumed that interactive meaning delivered by televised presidential adverting should serve for the process. In terms of visual resources, several social relations could be probed into. Moreover, the image-producer's hidden ideology, values and stances will further be illustrated in the following chapters:

Firstly, how the image-producers, being representatives of one side, treat their relations with the viewers;

Secondly, how the image-producers treat the relationship between the represented participants of their party and the viewers and the relationship between the represented participants of the other party and the viewers;

Thirdly, how the image-producers treat the relationship among all the represent participants and the circumstances around them in the picture.

Therefore, the above-mentioned framework on the analysis of interactive meaning could be reasonably applied to the analysis of the visual resources.

4.3.4 Compositional Meaning

Corresponding to textual meaning in SFG, compositional meaning in visual grammar functions as the connection, link the representational and interactive meaning as a whole. There are three compositional resources in the compositional meaning: information value, framing and salience.

Information Value

The role of any specific element in the integration is determined by the placement where it is put: left or right, top or down, center or margin, which has totally different meanings. According to Kress and Van Leeuwen, the placement, which is from left to right, constructs a structure of visual information as from given to new. That is to say, the element on the left suggests the given information, and right suggests new information. It is similar in functional grammar that the given information is common or apparent, while new information is questionable and disputed, as stated by Kress and Van Leeuwen in the following. For something to be given means that it is presented as something the viewer already knows, as a familiar and agreed-upon point of departure for the language. For something to be new means that it is presented as something the viewer does not know or not yet agreed upon, hence as something which must receive special attention (Kress & Van Leeuwen, 1996). Certainly, as a kind of meaning potential, in the specific image circumstance it will present specific profile. The top and down have different information values. The visual information is considered ideal if the element is placed on top, while the element placed down is considered as real.

In addition, the orientation of information value of the placement from the center to margin means the spread of the information from the dominant information to the subordinate information, and also has something to do with the differences of the culture.

The following diagram proposed by Kress & Van Leeuwen is the illustration of an information value system (Kress & Van Leeuwen, 1996):

Salience

The second process of the compositional meaning is salience. In pictures, elements have different importance regardless of their positions. And they tend to draw people's attention in different degrees. Some are more worthy of attention, while some blur into the background. This different degree of attention is referred to as salience. The given may be more salient than the New, for instance, or the New more salient than the given, or both may be equally salient. Whether an element is salient or not can be influenced by a number of factors: contrast, size, sharpness of focus, placement in the visual field or perspective, etc.

Figure 14　Dimension of Visual Space

Frame

The third important process of composition is framing. It refers to "the fact of whether there exist framing devices to connect or disconnect the elements in a picture". The framing devices can be either in weak form or in strong form. The stronger the framing of an element, the more the element is presented as a separate unit of information. The elements in a picture can be connected by similar colors, visual shape or vectors. They can also be disconnected by empty spaces, framing lines or discontinuities of color.

4.4　Image-text Relations

Image-text relations are another of the focus analyses in the present thesis. Early in the 1970s, Barthes's interest resulted in the analysis of the relationship between language and image generalized as "anchorage" "relay" and "illustration". Van Leeuwen (2005) puts forward his opinion on visual-verbal relations based on Barthes's original theory.

The relationship between the image and text can be roughly divided into two categories: elaboration and extension (Van Leeuwen, 2005).

The relationship between visual and verbal modes is internal and indispensable in terms of elaboration. Without the participants of either mode of the two, the discourses are confusing and misleading. Van Leeuwen (2005) further divides elaboration into two kinds: specification and explanation. Specification means that the image makes the text more specific, or vice versa. Explanation means that the text can illustrate the picture, or vice versa.

On the contrary, the relationships between verbal and visual modes is complementary in terms of extension. In other words, visual and verbal modes can cooperate and interact with each other with the construction of certain kinds of relationship between them. Three kinds of relationship, namely, similarity, contrast and complement have been identified (Van Leeuwen, 2005). Similarity means that the content of verbal modes is similar to that of visual modes; Contrast means that the content of the text differs from that of the image. Complement means that the content of the text adds further information to that of the image, or vice versa.

It can be seen that the selection of the two kinds of relationships depends on the decision on what and how information should be exposed to the viewers. Therefore, the interaction between them is ideologically-predominated.

4.5 Research Paradigm of the Study

As demonstrated in Figure 15, the present study first classified certain amount of US General Election Campaign Advertising into two categories, positive and negative advertising. It should be pointed out that for the elements in both positive and negative advertising are the same. The study on the variables of those two kinds, both in verbal and visual modes, should be the same, so that a comparative study can be made between them. It can be noted that they should follow the same theoretical framework for data analysis. In terms of theoretical framework, Halliday's SFG(1978) will be used for the analysis of verbal level, including both oral (transcript) and textual content and Kress & Van Leeuwen's VG(1996) used for the analysis of visual level. It also aims to build an integrated model for MCDA with its focus on the interaction between verbal and visual modes. The ultimate purpose of the data analysis is to reveal some distinctive features for the purpose of power and ideology.

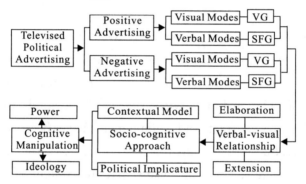

Figure 15   Research Paradigm of the Study

Chapter V

Research Methodology

5.1 Research Design

In light of the research questions proposed in the first chapter, the present study chose both qualitative and quantitative research methods, aiming to analyze the variables of different modes in meaning-making, probe into the internal relationships among them and to discuss power relation and manipulative force upon thought of the public through a corpus-based study on US General Election Campaign Advertising. The employment of qualitative research methods provided necessary theoretical basis for the classification, recognition, description and analysis of corpora from the perspective of different variables in both verbal and visual modes. By means of quantitative research method, statistics on distribution of the variables in terms of their frequency, mean value, maximum value and minimum value can be reliable references and verifications to the results, enhancing validity, objectivity and scientificity of the research. In addition, the introduction of computer-assistant methods into each step greatly facilitated data processing and analysis.

In the following, the research procedures, including corpus of the study, means of data gathering, means of data analysis in terms of qualitative research and correlated statistical instruments in terms of quantitative research will be elaborated step by step.

5.2 Corpus of the Study

The present study focused on corpus-based analysis on televised political advertising, taking US General Election Campaign Advertising from the year of 2008 to 2016 as its corpora. Since the study only focused on the English televised political advertising paid by candidates during the general campaign stage since the beginning of September to the first week in November, the scale of multimodal corpus was definable and controllable. A total of 206 televised presidential advertising pieces have been previously released by the US presidential candidates during campaign stages.

Table 10 shows the distribution of televised campaign advertising released by the presidential candidates in the most recent three cycles of the US presidential election:

Table 10　Distribution of Televised Campaign Advertising

Year of Election	Candidates	Number	Percentage
2008	Barack Obama(1)	41	19.90%
	John McCain	32	15.53%
2012	Barack Obama(2)	47	22.82%
	Mitt Romney	41	19.90%
2016	Hillary Clinton	27	13.11%
	Donald Trump	18	8.74%
Total		206	100%

Because of the asymmetric distribution of televised political advertising in each cycle of the presidential election, the same number of samples distributed in each year was adopted in the study. The reasons why 7 pieces of the televised campaign advertising for each candidate, to the utmost, were adopted in the present study for each president candidate according to the titles lie in the fact that only 18 pieces of televised campaign advertising had been released by Donald Trump as it is demonstrated in Table 11 and it

Chapter V Research Methodology

accounts for 20.39% of the 206 pieces collected for the data analysis, the proportion of which ensures the reliability of the analysis.

Table 11 demonstrates the number of samplings adopted for each candidate in the recent three cycles of election in the present data analysis:

Table 11 Numbers of Sampling

Year of Election	Candidates	Total Number	Number of Sampling	Percentage
2008	Barack Obama(1)	41	7	17.07%
	John McCain	32	7	21.88%
2012	Barack Obama(2)	47	7	14.89%
	Mitt Romney	41	7	17.07%
2016	Hillary Clinton	27	7	25.93%
	Donald Trump	18	7	38.89%
Total		206	42	20.39%

It should be pointed out that although there were five candidates involved in the presidential campaign in the three cycles, Barack Obama became the presidential candidates both in the years of 2008 and 2012. Therefore, 14 pieces of political advertising released by Barack Obama were involved in the present study, and 7 of them were released in 2008 and the other 7 were released in 2012.

All the verbal and visual data are available on the website DEMOCARCY IN ACTION and the related links on YouTube.

Table 12 provides the traceable website of televised political advertising from the year of 2008 to the year of 2016.

Table 12 Source of Verbal and Visual Data

Year of Election	URL
2008	http://p2008.org/ads08g2/tvads08g2.html
2012	http://www.p2012.org/ads3/adsgeneral.html
2016	http://www.p2016.org/adsg/adsgeneral.html

For more detailed information, a full list of names (Titles) and Premiere time of those campaign advertising are shown in the Appendices.

5.3　Data Gathering Procedures

For the sake of objectivity and reliability, the following steps and regulations were strictly conformed to:

Firstly, according to the list of the titles, 42 pieces of televised political advertising were randomly picked out from the website.

Secondly, the verbal corpora in the advertising consist of two forms: one refers to texts embedded in the advertising, and the other refers to utterances outside the motion pictures in the form of off-screen voice. The transcripts of both texts and utterances were retrieved directly from the website. For the sake of document retrieval and data notations, manual conversion into two file formats (doc. and txt.) was done simultaneously.

Thirdly, with regard to the collection of visual data, the conversion from a motion picture to series of static images was needed. In a piece of 30 seconds' televised presidential advertising, several static pictures were grasped and stored in the folder according to the sequence of different titles. Technically, in accordance with the fixed configuration, video processing software PotPlayer 64 bit was employed to capture and store images instantly and manually at the same time. The advertising was broadcasted without stop as Figure 16 shows its operational panel:

Figure 16　Operational Panel of PotPlayer 64 Bit

Chapter V   Research Methodology

Therefore, a cluster of pictures combined with the transcript of the words for each one were formed. Finally, in a folder named after the title is a short video, a transcript of the utterance and several high-quality screen captures as it is demonstrated in the following sample:

Title:"Something"

Date released: 30-second ad run in key states starting Oct. 31, 2008 (announced Oct. 30).

Figure 17. Sampling of Visual Data Collection

[Music]Male Announcer: Something is happening in America.

In small towns and big cities, People from every walk of life unite in common purpose.

A leader will bring us together.

Obama (clip from speech): We can choose hope over fear, and unity over division, the promise of change over the power of the status quo.

That's how we'll emerge from this crisis stronger and more prosperous...as one nation; and as one people.

Obama (voiceover): I'm Barack Obama, and I approve this message.

Figure 17   Sampling of Visual Data Collection

In all, 42 transcripts and more than 378 images were collected to form a small-scaled corpus base. After that, the data was grouped under the name of the presidential candidates in each cycle of the election year.

5.4 Encoding and Decoding of Data

In the process of data analysis, first and foremost, the linguistic and visual data were read and categorized according to the function of the advertising in the televised political adverting by the author through careful examining on the participants in the adverting. Then, for each piece, necessary manual coding was made on the variable from the perspective of verbal and visual modes respectively. After that, necessary calculation on the variables in each piece was done so as to discuss some internal relationship between two modes for the sake of manipulation of thought revealed by the analysis and statistics. The following steps should be followed:

Step One: Identification of the Function

The first step focused on who should speak and who should appear in the advertising. In other words, speakers or represented participants of two sides were defined first. For either side in the election, apart from the two candidates involved in the election, words or pictures in either positive or negative advertising were assigned to their supporters or opponents (off-screen voice included), beneficiaries or victims respectively, for the sake of presentation of advantages or benefits of one side on characters and policies in positive advertising, exposure ofshortcomings and harms of the other side in negative ones or emphasis of difficulties or problems to be dealt with. The study of the identity of the participants helped distinguish the positive advertising from negative advertising.

Table 13 shows that identity of the participants involved in the US televised campaign advertising.

Table 13 Participants Involved in the Televised Campaign Advertising

Who speaks		Who appears	
Positive Ads	Negative Ads	Positive Ads	Negative Ads
Candidates	Candidates	Candidates	Candidates
Supporters	Opponents	Supporters	Opponents
Third party	Third party	Third party	Third party
Announcer	Announcer	Film-maker	Film-maker

In terms of verbal modes, the main speakers in positive advertising were the presidential candidates and those who had released the advertising and their supporters. On the contrary, the main speakers in negative advertising were the candidates of the other side and their opponents. For the description of the concrete situation and circumstances, the third party without clear political stances was involved. Another main speaker in the advertising was the announcer or known as off-screen voice, who naturally spoke for the owner of the adverting. In terms of visual modes, the participants were easier to be identified. For the positive advertising, only the candidate and their supports appeared in it. For the negative advertising, the candidate of the other side and their opponent appeared in it. Similar to the verbal modes, the third party possibly appeared or a pure description of the atmosphere was made by the film-maker with no participant in it.

Therefore, the identification of the participant was a reliable indication to the functional categorization of the political adverting. Data categorization in the present study primarily followed Benoit's tradition. All the linguistic and non-linguistic data were categorized into two kinds, depending on communicative intentions. Different producers, contents and time would not be taken into consideration in this step. Two notations were defined previously: <+> means acclaim, <-> meaning attack. Naturally, the pictures along with the words were further categorized in terms of its function.

Step Two: Analysis of Verbal Modes Under the Guidance of Systemic-functional Grammar

In terms of ideational function, the present study focused on transitivity and lexical choices. In this qualitative aspect of the paper, six processes were identified, documented and analyzed. The number of each type in every piece of adverting was counted. For its distribution in both positive and negative advertising was a significant indication of meaning-potentials in terms of SFG. The largest proportion among them was exemplified in the discussion part, revealing certain kinds of buried meanings of power and ideology.

The following are the codes for the variables of transitivity:

 Material Process:<+> Obama: We can choose hope over fear, and unity over division, the promise of change over the power of the status quo.

 Relational process:<+> Obama: That's how we'll emerge from this crisis stronger and more prosperous…as one nation; and as one people.

 Mental process:<+> Obama: We all know the answer to that.

 Verbal process:<+> Male Announcer: Barack Obama says both extremes are wrong.

 Existential Process:<+> Obama: There are better days ahead.

In terms of interpersonal function, the study focused on the mood system, modality system, personal pronouns and quotations. For the mood system, the information of "demand" and "offer" was distinguished via the choice of sentence structures; it focused on the different values of modal verbs exposing one's attitude to the modality systems; as for personal pronouns and quotations it concentrated on the construction of individual or collective social identities in social interaction, considering its importance in the establishment of social relations.

The following are the codes for the variables of mood system:

 Indicative: <+> Announcer: His grandfather fought in Patton's army.

 Interrogative: <+> Biden: Have you seen this ad questioning what kind of people Barack Obama would appoint?

 Imperative: <+> Announcer: Keep your employer paid coverage!

The following are the codes for the variables of modality system:

 Modal verbs: <+> Obama: I believe we need to fund our schools, but that no money can take the place of a parent taking responsibility for their child.

The following are the codes for the variables of personal pronouns:

Chapter V   Research Methodology

Personal Pronouns: <+> Barack Obama: How will I pay for these priorities? First, we've got to stop spending ten billion dollars a month in Iraq—while they run up a surplus. I'll end this war responsibly, so we can invest here at home.

The following are the codes for quotations:

Quotations: <+> The independent Tax Policy Center says Obama offers middle class tax cuts three times as big as McCain's.

It should be noted that the words in quotation always collaborated with verbal modes in televised political adverting. Therefore, only indirect quotations were documented and analyzed in this step.

Figure 18 shows the application of meta-functions to the analysis of linguistic data:

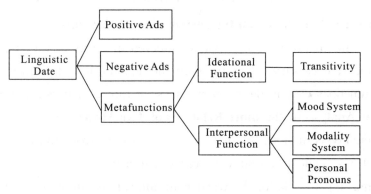

Figure 18   Procedures of Verbal Data Analysis

Step Three: Analysis of Visual Modes Under the Guidance of Visual Grammar

As regards to the analysis of visual resources, data analysis was based on functional categorizations. The study adopted visual grammar as its theoretical framework for the analysis of interactive meaning.

As for the interactive meaning, attitudes and social relations among the participants inside and out of the image (image-maker and viewers) were analyzed from four aspects: contact, size of frame, perspective and modality markers.

Under the guidance of visual grammar, the analysis on the clusters was made from the perspectives of different variables in two kinds of televised political advertising. After that, necessary calculation and comparison of the distribution of the variables were made.

Figure 19 shows the procedures of visual data analysis from the guidance of functional approach and visual grammar:

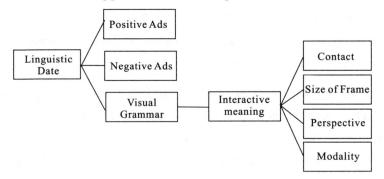

Figure 19　Procedures of Visual Data Analysis

Step Four: The Calculation on the Distribution of Variables

After the qualitative study was conducted in terms of the coding of all the variables, necessary calculations on the distribution of them in terms of different functions were made to get statistics for future analysis quantitatively.

Step Five: Analysis of the Inner Relations of Two Modes

The analysis of both linguistic and visual data from the perspective of two functions made it possible to carry out a comparative and correlated study regarding to relation between communicative intentions and semiotic choices. The next step was to explore the inner relations of the two modes under the basis of the previous analysis so as to expose discourse power and ideology. For the facility of data analysis, the image-text relations between visual and verbal modes were analyzed from two perspectives: specification in elaboration and complement in extension in the present study.

Step Six: Validation of Manual Coding Process

Three professors with Doctoral Degree in the field of language teaching and learning helped to validate the data gathered from the manual coding processes in the present research. For the data doubted by the validators, several actions were taken by the author to verify and correct them: Firstly, a thorough investigation on the incorrect data was done. Secondly, discussion about the understanding and explanation of the coding with

Chapter Ⅴ　Research Methodology

professors was finished. Finally, some necessary corrections on the incorrect coding were completed.

5.5　Statistical Instrument

Regarding the linguistic data processing, computer-assisted techniques were accessible. For word and clause searching and counting, AntConc, a freeware, multiplatform tool for carrying out corpus linguistics research and data-driven learning, will be introduced into the research. It is well-known for its user-friendly interface and convenient operation. Moreover, not only can it realize all the functions of Word Smith, but also contribute a lot to the research field of corpus linguistics.

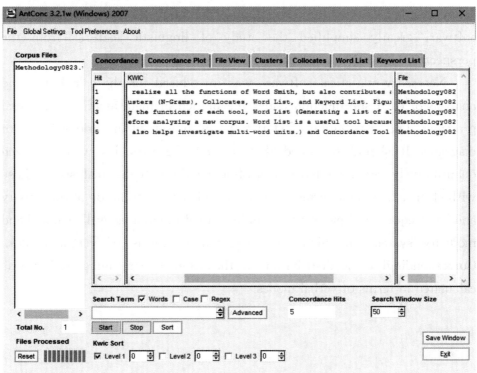

Figure 20　Operation Interface of Antconc

As shown in Figure 20, AntConc contains seven tools that can be accessed either by clicking on their "tabs" in the tool window, or using the function keys F1 to F7, relevant to seven linguistic retrieval tools: Concordance tool, Concordance Plot Tool, File View Tool, Clusters, Collocate, Word List and Key Word List.

With respect to the present study, the function of Word List was first used to get the general information on the distribution of words, including lexical density, numbers of word types and numbers of word token. In addition, a list of words was generated in a frequency order. Later, phrases and clauses related to a certain word were positioned and sorted in the file with the help of Concordance, used toform an index of word clusters. For example, all the modal verbs were sorted out in terms of their values; personal pronouns were categorized in terms of their different identities and references. It facilitated the retrieval of certain linguistic data. Therefore, the software greatly simplified the study of linguistic features from the perspective of three meta-functions.

Necessary statistical software was introduced for the calculation and analysis of each sub-function under the branch of meta-functions or visual grammar. The distribution of statistics was presented in various forms of diagrams. It should be noted that not all the variables were analyzed quantitatively. Statistics have been obtained through the analysis of those with clear taxonomy in terms of SFG and VG. The distribution of transitivity and the frequency of passive voice in ideational function as well as mood and modality systems in SFG were counted in terms of verbal modes. Correspondingly, the distribution of the interactive meaning in VG was calculated in terms of verbal modes.

Chapter VI

Distribution of Verbal and Visual Modes

The present study, on the basis of functional classification of televised political advertising, aimed to focus on the analysis of verbal data from the perspective of SFG as well as visual data analysis from the perspective of VG. Statistics on the distribution of variables in both of the two modes can help to expose the internal relationship between two modes for meaning-making, further mirror the buried meaning of power and ideology. For the facilitation and objectivity of the study, therefore, results on the functional distribution of corpus were first presented and then results on the distribution of variables in both verbal and visual modes are shown respectively in this section.

6.1 Functional Distribution of Corpus

42 pieces of televised political advertising have been randomly selected in the present research. For more detailed information, a full list of names of those campaign advertising is shown in the Appendices.

For the purpose of winning more support from the potential voters, two directions of meaning-making have been identified. The candidate himself may be the focus of the advertising or the opponent of the candidate may be the other focus of the advertising. No matter in positive or negative advertising, the candidate himself will make a self-introduction and approve the message at the beginning or the end of the advertising. Therefore, the political stance of the advertising is clear. Thus, all the 42 pieces can be divided into two categories in terms of its political intentions: one is positive advertising and the other is negative advertising through the analysis of the identities of both speakers and characters based on Benoit's functional approach to political advertising.

Table 14 shows the distribution of the different identities of the candidates in terms of the verbal and visual modes in the political advertising released by Barack Obama1 and John McCain in the year of 2008.

Table 14 Functional Distribution of Campaign Ads in 2008

Candidate A Barack Obama			Candidate B John McCain		
Titles	Positive	Negative	Titles	Positive	Negative
Something	+		Freedom	+	
His Choice		-	Charlie Crist ads	+	
Defining Moment	+		Fight	+	
Unravel		-	Tiny		-
One Word		-	Ladies and Gentlemen		-
Same Path	+		Foundation	+	
Figured	+		Education		-
Totality	4	3	Totality	4	3

Table 15 shows the distribution of the different identities of the candidates in terms of the verbal and visual modes in the political advertising released by Barack Obama and Mitt Romney in the year of 2012.

Chapter VI Distribution of Verbal and Visual Modes

Table 15 Functional Distribution of Campaign Ads in 2012

Candidate A Barack Obama			Candidate B Mitt Romney		
Titles	Positive	Negative	Titles	Positive	Negative
Solid	+		Iowa Newspaper Agree	+	
Character	+		The Clear Path	+	
Determination	+		The Obama Plan		-
Decision		-	Way of Life		-
My Job		-	The Romney Plan	+	
To Us		-	Failing American Workers		-
Won't Say		-	Give Me a Break		-
Totality	3	4	Totality	3	4

Table 16 shows the distribution of the different identities of the candidates in terms of the verbal and visual modes in the political advertising released by Hillary Clinton and Donald Trump in the year of 2016.

Table 16 Functional Distribution of Campaign Ads in 2016

Candidate A Hillary Clinton			Candidate B Donald Trump		
Titles	Positive	Negative	Titles	Positive	Negative
Tomorrow	+		Unfit		-
We are America		-	United	+	
What He Believes		-	Corruption		-
Family First	+		Rebuilding the American Dream	+	
A Place for Everyone	+		Laura		-
Measure	+		Dangerous		-
Low Opinion		-	Listening	+	
Totality	4	3	Totality	3	4

Table 17 shows the functional distribution of televised political advertising for each candidate.

Table 17 Total Numbers of Positive and Negative Campaign Ads for Each Candidates

Year of Election	Candidates	Total Number	Positive	Percentage	Negative	Percentage
2008	Barack Obama[1]	7	4	57.14%	3	42.86%
	John McCain	7	4	57.14%	3	42.86%
2012	Barack Obama[2]	7	3	42.86%	4	57.14%
	Mitt Romney	7	3	42.86%	4	57.14%
2016	Hillary Clinton	7	4	57.14%	3	42.86%
	Donald Trump	7	3	42.86%	4	57.14%
Totality		42	21	50%	21	50%

It can be noted that, among 42 pieces, the total number of positive televised political adverting is equal to the number of negative ones, though the distribution for different candidates in the three cycles of presidential election is different.

6.2 Verbal Modes Analysis

6.2.1 Ideational Meaning of Verbal Modals

Transitivity

The analysis of transitivity is an important and useful tool in CDA. According to Simpson & Mayr (2010), the analysis of agency and action should be analyzed in three aspects of meaning-making in a process, namely, actors, processes and circumstance. Different verbs taken into consideration, there are six types of processes: material process, relational process, mental process, verbal process, existential process and behavioral process being identified and counted in the analysis. The occurrence of six processes in both verbal and visual modes noted are manually coded and accounted. Its distribution is shown in Table 18.

Table 18 reveal the distribution of six processes in both positive and negative televised political advertising respectively.

Chapter VI Distribution of Verbal and Visual Modes

Table 18 Distribution of Six Processes of Transitivity

Transitivity Process	Positive Televised Political Advertising		Negative Televised Political Advertising	
	Frequency	Percentage	Frequency	Percentage
Material Process	276	65.56%	124	53.44%
Relational Process	98	23.28%	60	25.57%
Mental Process	38	9.03%	62	15.65%
Verbal Process	5	1.19%	14	5.34%
Existential Process	4	0.95%	1	0.38%
Behavioral Process	0	0	0	0
Totality	421	100%	261	100%

Statistics in Table 18 reveals that the first two kinds, including material and relational processes account for the largest proportion in both positive and negative advertising.

For each candidate, their choices of different processes are varied. The distribution of six processes in positive advertising is shown in Table 19.

Table 19 Employment of Transitivity in Positive Ads for Each Candidates

Process	Material	Relational	Mental	Verbal	Existential	Behavioral
Obama	90	20	11	1	0	0
Mccain	38	12	2	1	0	0
Obama2	36	16	5	1	2	0
Romney	34	15	2	0	1	0
Clinton	58	30	17	2	0	0
Trump	20	5	1	0	1	0
Totality	276	98	38	5	4	0

Table 19 reveals that more material processes occur in Obama's positive advertising, while Clinton prefers to use mental processes comparing with other candidates.

The distribution of six processes for each candidate in negative advertising is demonstrated in Table 20.

Table 20　Employment of Transitivity in Negative Ads for Each Candidate

Process	Material	Relational	Mental	Verbal	Existential	Behavioral
Obama	16	7	8	1	0	0
Mccain	13	7	9	2	0	0
Obama 2	17	8	13	3	0	0
Romney	30	11	6	3	1	0
Clinton	25	19	20	5	0	0
Trump	23	8	7	0	0	0
Totality	124	60	60	14	1	0

Table 20 reveals that more material processes occur in Romney's negative advertising, while more relational and mental processes appear in Clinton's.

6.2.2　Interpersonal Meaning of Verbal Modes

Mood

Mood expresses the speech function; the underlying pattern of organization is the exchange system of giving or demanding information or good-and-services, which determine the four basic speech functions of statement, question, offer and command (Halliday, 1985). As mentioned above, the mood system basically consists of the subject and finite, the exchange of which plays an essential role in carrying out the interpersonal function of the clause. There are three main categories of clauses in the mood system of clauses, namely, declarative clauses, interrogative clauses and imperative clauses, the choice of which will be determined by complicated factors, such as the social status of the speakers or the communicative goals. The study on the distribution of the mood systems can expose the absolute dominance of power which is one of the focuses in CDA. However, it is also because of inequality in the distribution of power in social construction that the mood system is not enough to cover all the functions language have to establish and sustain the asymmetrical relationship between speakers and hearers. Table 21 reveals the number of the mood system in both positive and

Chapter VI Distribution of Verbal and Visual Modes

negative televised political advertising respectively distributed in the selected materials.

Table 21 Distribution of Mood System

Interpersonal Function Mood System	Positive Ads		Negative Ads	
	Frequency	Percentage	Frequency	Percentage
Declarative	270	89.11%	205	86.86%
Interrogative	14	4.62%	13	5.51%
Imperative	17	5.61%	18	7.63%
Exclamatory	2	0.66%	0	0.00%
Totality	303	100%	236	100%

For the mood systems, the ratios in both positive and negative ones are nearly the same. Among the 539 pieces of definable clauses, the number of declarative clauses approaches to 90% of the total number, accounting for 89.11% in the positive advertising and 86.86% in the negative advertising respectively. The result is coincident to the findings in the related studies that US citizens do not care about politics and lack of necessary informationand knowledge on politics, especially, on the characters and future policies possessed by the candidates (Delli, Carpini & Keeter, 1996).

For the occurrences of mood system for each candidate, Table 22 and Table 23 present the number of difference sentence patterns in both positive and negative advertising.

Table 22 Employment of Mood System in Positive Ads for Each Candidate

Mood System	Declarative	Imperative	Interrogative
Obama	67	0	4
Mccain	46	6	3
Obama 2	34	4	1
Romney	36	2	0
Clinton	53	5	6
Trump	34	0	0
Totality	270	17	14

Statistics in Table 22 reveals that declarative clauses account for the largest proportion in Obama's positive advertising in 2008. McCain uses more imperative clauses than other candidates, while Clinton prefers to use interrogative ones.

Table 23   Employment of Mood System in Negative Ads for Each Candidate

Mood System	Declarative	Imperative	Interrogative
Obama	24	2	0
Mccain	28	0	3
Obama 2	31	2	1
Romney	34	2	4
Clinton	59	11	2
Trump	29	1	3
Totality	205	18	13

According to Table 23, Clinton most frequently employs declarative and imperative clauses in her negative. Comparatively, Romney is more inclined to interrogative clauses.

Modality

As it is mentioned above, various modal auxiliary verbs are frequently used in political discourses for various communicative goals, such as determination, command, proposal, obligation, reprimand etc. and thus, the power relationship can be constructed through the selection of different modal auxiliaries. According to Halliday and Matthiessen (2004), modality involves "degrees and scales", and it is classified into "high, median and low value". With the help of Antconc, three kinds of modal auxiliaries are defined and counted in the present studies in terms of their scales and values of probabilities and obligations, whose distributions are shown in Table 24.

Table 24 shows the distribution of modal auxiliaries employed in positive and negative advertising in the campaign advertising.

Chapter VI Distribution of Verbal and Visual Modes

Table 24 Distribution of Modal Auxiliaries

Value	Modal Auxiliaries	Positive Ads		Negative Ads	
		Frequency	Percentage	Frequency	Percentage
High	have/has (got) to	7	14.1%	4	14.81%
	must	1		1	
	need	4		3	
Median	will	50	60.9%	19	62.96%
	would	3		12	
	should	2		3	
	ought	1		0	
Low	can	23	25%	5	22.22%
	could	0		6	
	might	0		1	
Totality		91	100%	54	100%

According to Table 24, it can be concluded that the distribution of modal verbs indicates that those with median and low values, such as *will*, *can*, *would*, *should*, *ought* and etc. are more preferable than others with high values, namely, have (has) to, must and need in both positive and negative televised political advertising.

Personal Pronouns

As it has been mentioned above, personal pronouns with different range of deixis are noteworthy indicators of interpersonal relationships in political discourses, its choices in various contexts helping to illustrate one's political stance as well as to establish certain social relations among the characters within and beyond discourses.

Table 25 shows the distribution of personal pronouns employed in positive and negative advertising in the campaign advertising.

Table 25 Distribution of Personal Pronoun in Positive and Negative Ads

Ranges	Personal Pronoun	Positive ads			Negative ads		
		Frequency	Total Number	Percentage	Frequency	Total Number	Percentage
First-Person Pronoun (Plural.)	we	67	119	37.07%	13	21	10.3%
	our	41			4		
	us	11			4		
First-Person Pronoun (Singular)	I	103	125	38.94%	75	83	40.9%
	my	16			5		
	me	6			3		
Second-Person Pronoun	you	27	41	12.77%	31	40	19.7%
	your	14			9		
Third-person Pronoun	they/he/she	17	36	11.21%	25	59	29.1%
	their/his/her	11			20		
	Them/him	8			14		
Totality		321	321	100%	203	203	100%

Statistics in Table 25 reveal that singular forms of first-person pronouns are most frequently employed in both positive and negative advertising. However, it is notable that more inclusive pronouns are employed in positive advertising while more exclusive pronouns appear in negative advertising in terms of their proportions.

6.3 Visual Modes Analysis

6.3.1 Interactive Meaning of Visual Modes

Similar to interpersonal function in SFG, different interactive meanings can also be realized by the selection of contact, size of frame, perspective and modality.

Chapter VI Distribution of Verbal and Visual Modes

Contact

Following Halliday's tradition, four functions of the Mood system can be recognized in interpersonal functions; only two functions can be revealed in terms of interactive meaning: one is "demand image"; the other "offer image". The only way to differentiate "demand image" from "offer image" is whether direct eye contact in the image can be perceived by the receivers. For the "demand image", the characters in the picture will have constant eye contact with the reactors, waiting for their feedback, such as approval, admission, support, denial and etc., while the receivers or viewers being passive observers, are exclusive in the "offer image". Therefore, the advertisers' selection of contacts aims to construct certain kinds of social relations between an image and its receivers.

Table 26 shows the distribution of contact in both positive and negative advertising in 378 pieces of pictures captured from the campaign advertising.

Table 26 Distribution of Contact in Positive and Negative Ads

Interactive Meaning Contact System	Positive Ads		Negative Ads	
	Frequency	Percentage	Frequency	Percentage
Demand Image	55	29.1%	26	13.7%
Offer Image	134	70.9%	163	86.3%
Totality	189	100%	189	100%

As shown in Table 26, "offer images" are more preferable than "demand images" in both positive and negative campaign advertising. The result is congruent to the analysis of verbal data that declarative clauses account for the largest proportion in mood system for the same intention of sending information.

Size of Frame

For another main focus of interactive meaning, the analysis of size of frame can reveal degrees of social distance between the characters in the image and their viewers. In turn, it is a contrivable method of constructing certain kinds of social ties and expressing different attitude by making different selections, namely, long shot, medium shot and close-up shot.

Table 27 shows the distribution of the size of the frame in 317 pieces of pictures with recognizable characters captured from the campaign advertising, 169 pieces in positive advertising and 148 pieces in negative ones.

Table 27　Distribution of Size of Frame in Positive and Negative Ads

Interactive Meaning Size of Frame	Positive Ads		Negative Ads	
	Frequency	Percentage	Frequency	Percentage
Close-up	53	31.36%	71	47.97%
Medium	97	57.40%	60	40.54%
Long	19	11.24%	17	11.49%
Totality	169	100%	148	100%

Statistics in Table 27 reveals that differentiation on the choices of "size of frame" exists between positive ads and negative ads. The medium shots are more preferred by the advertisers in positive ads; the close-up shots are more adopted in negative ones.

Perspective

Perspective refers to the angles from which the participants in the images can be seen by the viewers. Two kinds of perspectives will be analyzed: the horizontal and vertical. Horizontal angle consists of frontal angle and oblique angle. It determines how the viewers are involved in the images.

Table 28 shows the distribution of horizontal perspectives in 317 pieces of images with recognizable characters captured from the campaign advertising.

Table 28　Distribution of Horizontal Perspectives in Positive and Negative advertising

Interactive Meaning Horizontal Perspectives	Positive Ads		Negative Ads	
	Frequency	Percentage	Frequency	Percentage
Frontal	98	60.1%	46	35.1%
Oblique	65	39.9%	85	64.9%
Totality	163	100%	131	100%

Notable differences have been revealed in terms of the distribution of perspectives in both positive and negative advertising. Statistics in Table 28

Chapter VI Distribution of Verbal and Visual Modes

show that the advertisers are inclined to choose frontal angles instead of oblique ones in positive advertising while more oblique angles are selected in negative ones.

Modality Markers

Similar to modal auxiliaries in interpersonal meaning, such variables of modality markers as color saturation and contextualization are related in degrees of certainty, authenticity and possibility. Generally speaking, the more naturalistic the image looks, the more authentic and possible the meaning is. In other words, the selection of modality markers also create kinds of meaning potential with metaphorical meaning indicating the producer's attitude and cognition towards the world. Therefore, the analysis of such modality markers as color saturation and contextualization in televised political advertising can be a significant way of studying "political implicatures".

Color Saturation

It should be admitted that values of color saturation are not as definable as those of modal auxiliaries in verbal modes as the perception of color saturation possessed by human being is biologically dominated. Depending on "sensory truth" proposed by Machin & Mayr (2012), color saturation consists of two kinds, naturalistic and non-naturalistic ones. Two variables in color saturation have been recognized and counted as shown in Table 29.

Table 29 shows the distribution of color saturation in both positive and negative advertising.

Table 29 Distribution of Color Saturation in Positive and Negative Ads

Modality Markers	Values	Positive Ads		Negative Ads	
		Frequency	Percentage	Frequency	Percentage
Color Saturation	Naturalistic	173	91.53%	52	27.51%
	Non-naturalistic	16	8.47%	137	72.49%
Totality		189	100%	189	100%

As shown in Table 29 a notable polarization on the distribution of color saturation reveals that naturalisti ccolors are more preferable, accounting for 91.

53% in positive televised political advertising, while more non-naturalistic colors are adopted in negative ones, accounting for 72.49%.

Contextualization

Contextualization is relevant to the truth values as it is obvious that the more information is clearly revealed in a piece of advertising, the more authentic it becomes in it. In addition, degrees of articulation in contextualization lead to the shift of focus between foregrounding and backgrounding.

Table 30 shows the distribution of contextualization in both positive and negative advertising.

Table 30 Distribution of Contextualization in Positive and Negative Ads

Modality Markers	Values	Positive Ads		Negative Ads	
		Frequency	Percentage	Frequency	Percentage
Contextualization	Naturalistic	95	50.3%	41	21.7%
	Blurred	68	26%	101	53.4%
	Absent	26	13.7%	47	24.9%
Totality		189	100%	189	100%

Demonstrated in Table 30, the largest amount of naturalistic contexts with high values appears positive. By contrast, blurred contexts with lower modality are most favorable in negative advertising.

Chapter VII

Meaning-making in Verbal-Visual Interaction

7.1 Meaning-making in Ideational Function

7.1.1 On Transitivity

Though the number of both kinds of televised political advertising adopted in the present research is the same, it can be noted that more processes appear in positive televised political advertising than negative ones as more time and discourse power has been given to the former ones for the reason that the advertisers should take full advantage of time to make self-promotions in the advocacy of their future policy and shaping their characters. The distribution of discourse power can be reflected by the numbers of word tokens in both positive and negative advertising. According to Statistics, 3,091 word tokens have been hit in the 21 pieces of positive advertising, and only 2,161 word tokens hit in the same amount of negative advertising.

For the data randomly selected, a traditional way of political advertising is comparatively long, in which the candidates themselves talk to the camera or audience about his plans has been frequently employed in positive advertising, though most of the advertising, either positive or negative, lasts in less than 30 seconds. For the sake of verbal modes, clear explanation or direct appealing can be made to potential voters. For example, In Data 3 (in Appendices), Barack Obama, sitting in front of the camera, answered the two questions of whether the US would be better and how to lift US economy and restore its place in the world step by step with a list of the same sentence structure " I will do … ", if he could be elected to be the President:

> Obama: Here's what I'll **do** as President. To deal with our current emergency, I'll **launch** a rescue plan for the middle class. That **begins with** a tax cut for ninety-five percent of working Americans. If you **have** a job, **pay** taxes and **make** less than two hundred thousand dollars-a-year, you'll **get** a tax cut. I'll **end** the tax breaks for companies that ship our jobs overseas, and **give** them to companies that create jobs here in America. And I'll **make** low-cost loans available to small businesses.

It seems to be a simple, effective and favorable way for Barack Obama to propagandize his future policy in positive advertising. In Obama's second running for US president, the similar examples can be found. In Data 11, the advertising begins with Obama's voiceover with stock footage and his direct talk to the camera for the rest part. The adverting ties in with the 20-page booklet the campaign released on the same day. It is known that more of this type of advertising and less of the Romney attack might help his campaign; there are quite a few big questions he has not addressed much to date in the campaign, such as how he'll move beyond partisan gridlock, implementation of the health care law, and so forth.

Similarly, Hillary Clinton in Data 15 entitled "Tomorrow" logically clarifying a few things to her potential voters one day before Election Day, lays out the choice in this election and the type of president she wants to be for the entire country. In such a personal and positive closing message, Clinton makes the case that people are rejecting a campaign "defined by fear and division" and choosing one that is "hopeful and inclusive" by saying:

> Our core values **are being tested** in this election.
> But everywhere I go, people **are refusing** to be defined by fear and division.

Chapter Ⅶ Meaning-making in Verbal-Visual Interaction

> Look, we all **know** we've **come through** some hard economic times and we **have some pretty big changes, but I believe** in our people. (Tomorrow)

On the contrary, the negative political advertising is comparatively short, brief and obscure with the purpose of exposing the deficiency of the policies and poor characters of the candidates of the other side. Linguistic features should be related to the expression of such negative emotions as indifference, arrogance, dissatisfaction, disappointment, emotions through concrete descriptions made by image-producers.

It can be noted that discrepancy on primary tones and attitudes on positive and negative advertising can be figured out. The positive ones should be more rational, objective, and affirmative while the negative ones should be more emotional, subjective and discredited. As a result, comparison on the distributions of six processes in verbal and visual modes reveals that preferences are given to material and relational processes. However, more mental processes are employed in negative advertising than those in positive ones.

The material processes, known as the process of doing, refer to the representation of outer experience. According to Halliday (1985), the choice of the material processes expresses the notion that some entity "does" something—which may be done to some other entity. Statistics indicate that in both positive and negative televised political advertising, material processes occur more frequently than other processes, accounting for 65.56% and 53.44% of the total number of processes respectively. The reason is that in any televised political adverting, the owner of the advertising has to make their speeches sound persuasive and reasonable to the hearers. Therefore, the material processes are relatively proper in terms of their structures. Being the candidates for the future American president, they had to employ the most powerful, objective and persuasive way to convey their perspectives so as to let their hearer firmly believe that what they had said was absolutely true and reliable.

The outstanding features of those positive and negative advertising in the application of material process is that it starts with or ends with the candidate's ritual, authentic assured words by saying "I approved this message" in each piece, which reach to 43 times in total as Hillary Clinton in Data 15 repeated this sentence at the end of the advertising.

 e. g. <u>I</u>   <u>approved</u>   <u>this message.</u>
    Actor   Process   Goal

 Three aspects in a material process can be definitely perceived by the audience, which can create an effect that reliable information in the adverting is reconfirmed by a powerful person on his/her own who could be competent to be the leader of the country.

 The concrete action can also be detected by the audience in the material process. On one hand, the candidates had to emphasize what they had done and what they would do for the country and for the voters in the positive advertising; on the other hand, they had to point out that what negative effects would be produced if their opponents could be selected. For example: Noting the Buffett and Powell endorsements and referring on screen to the "Obama Economic Plan", Data 1 makes a very concrete elaboration on the situation the voters have been involved in and the bright future they can choose if Obama can be elected as the leader by using a series of verbs, such as, happening, unite, bring, choose and emerge from.

  <u>Male Announcer</u>: Something's **happening** in America. In small towns and big cities, People from every walk of life **unite** in common purpose. A leader who'll **bring** us together.

  <u>Obama (clip from speech)</u>: We can **choose** hope over fear, and unity over division, the promise of change over the power of the status quo.

  That's how we'll **emerge from** this crisis stronger and more prosperous as one nation and as one people.

 Data 7 is a typical example for the significance of using material processes in political advertising. McCain exposed the incompetence of the previous government and the tremendous damage and loss done to the country's economy in the past few years.

  <u>McCain</u>: The last eight years **haven't worked** very well, have they? Washington is **making** it **worse-bankrupting** us with their spending.

Chapter Ⅶ Meaning-making in Verbal-Visual Interaction

>They **refuse** common sense solutions for energy independence.
>So every day, we **send** billions to the Middle East. (Data 7)

Later, he emphasized his plans on how to solve those problems and the benefits brought to the voters in the next four years. A material result and consequence can be perceived by the audience because of the processes. For example:

>McCain: We **need** a new direction, and I have a plan.
>Your savings. We'll **rebuild** them.
>Your investments. They'll **grow** again.
>Energy. We'll **drill** here and we'll **create** a renewable energy economy.
>(Data 7)

In those examples, three aspects of a process have been clearly expressed. The actor element is the pronoun "we" that will carry out those significant action; the goal is the topic listed ahead of time, such as **saving, investment and energy.** Later, the beneficiaries or receivers are definitely expressed because of those actions by using those material processes in the following example:

>McCain : Lower taxes and less spending will **protect** your job and **create** new ones.
>That'll **restore** our country. (Data 7)

Relational process is also known as processes of being (Halliday, 1985), which consists of three kinds of sub-types in relational process, namely, intensive, circumstantial and possessive process. In the intensive process the two nominal groups are linked by the typical word "be" or the other verbs functioning as "be" in terms of grammar, such as *become, turn, remain, stay, seem, appear, end up, turn out, look, sound, smell, feel taste*, etc. In the possessive process, the relationship between two nominal groups is one of ownership with the words *have, own, contain, include, involve, comprise* or *belong to* connecting them. When circumstance functions as a process, it is expressed by the verb, e. g. , concern, last and so on, which is known as circumstantial process.

In general, the relational process explicitly presents the characteristics of property and relation, which sounds objective. Therefore, it is very common in political discourses. It is a less powerful but more direct and distinct way to express a definition, truth or fact. For example:

McCain: You, the American workers, **are** the best in the world. (Data 8)

John Glemn: And you know he **means** what he says. That **is** the Ohio way. (Data 10)

Romney: The President's path will **mean** continuing declining in take-home pay. The President's path **means** 20 million people out of work struggling for a good job. (Data 13)

Announcer: It **is** not the change we need. (Data 23)

Announcer: Romney **is** not the solution. He **is** the problem. (Data 30)

A relational process of making self-introduction to the owner of the advertising coexists with the material process of their approval of the information in the advertising. Similarly, such a simple and precise way of identity construction can help to consolidate his power and confidence via the creation of a bright and clear public image for the potential voters.

In addition, the relational processes continually appeared in the advertising for the sake of description of the current situation and elaboration of the candidates' future policy. For example, the possessive processes, a sub-type of relational processes using have, has and had, etc. could send the message to his hearers that the candidate, confronted with incredible challenges, was ready and able to lead this country with a blueprint in his minds in positive advertising. On the contrary, the employment of the possessive processes with negative words indicates that their opponent can send a message that their rivals haven't been capable of leading the country. All the candidates prefer to use possessive processes. For example:

Obama: On taxes, John McCain and I **have** very different ideas. (Data 3)

Biden: We're going to **have** an international crisis…to test the mettle of this guy. (Data 26)

Clinton: Because we all **have** a role to play in building a stronger, fairer

Chapter Ⅶ Meaning-making in Verbal-Visual Interaction

America. (Data 15)

Announcer: It takes a builder to rebuild the American Dream, and Donald Trump **has** the blueprint. (Data 20)

Trump: You can't lead this nation if you **have** such a low opinion for its citizens. (Data 37)

Hillary Clinton doesn't **have** the fortitude, strength or stamina to lead in our world. (Data 42)

The mental processes relate to the processes of sensing, such as feeling, thinking and seeing, which are marked with those verbs showing the conscious activities of human beings. A mental process should consist of senser and phenomenon which are comparable to the two participants in the material process with a verb inserted between them, the senser is the conscious being that is feeling, thinking or seeing, the phenomenon is that which is sensed (Halliday, 1985) and the verb can be sub-divided into three categories: ① perception (seeing, hearing, etc.), ② affection (liking, fearing, etc.) and ③ cognition (thinking, knowing, understanding, etc.).

In discourses, the use of mental process may be completely different from that of material process, as mental process, being a kind of conscious activity, is evident that the former will be more subjective rather than objective. The mental process often reflects the sensor's opinion or attitude towards what has happened. Statistics in Table 18 indicate that mental processes are more preferable in negative advertising than positive advertising for the reason that the frequent use of mental processes by their rivals in the negative ones may indicate that those candidates, to be the leader of the most powerful country, lack necessary leadership. They are sentimental rather than rational, artificial rather than trustworthy, vacillating rather than decisive. In the 2016 American Presidential Election, Hillary Clinton deliberately quoted Trump's words in an audio clip to show his incompetence, unsteadiness in leading the nation by using mental processes such as *look*, *like*, *don't know*, *love*, *remember*, *hate* and etc. in a sequence along with the first-person pronoun *I* as its senser. For example:

Trump (audio clips):

I'd **look** her right in that fat ugly face of hers.

He's a war hero cause he was captured; I **like** people that weren't captured, okay?

You got to **see** this guy, oh, I don't **know** what I said, ah, I don't **remember**.

I'd **like** to punch him in the face.

I **love** war in a certain way. (Data 36)

Trump: Oh, I don't **know** what I said, ah; I don't **remember**.

Trump: He is a war hero because he was captured. I **like** people that weren't captured, okay, I **hate** to tell you.

Trump: I'd **like** to punch him in the face. (Data 38)

Therefore, it is not advisable for politicians to use so many mental processes on the ground that such a process is treated to be irrational, subjective, artificial, uncertain and too cautious, which, in turn, influences the authority and credibility of the speeches. In other words, the speaker's ability of controlling his hearers may be reduced.

In addition, direct quotations of mental processes given by the rivals of the candidates in the negative advertising imply that those speakers try to gain an insight into the feelings or states of minds of certain participants and impose their ideology upon the public. For example:

Romney: There are 47 percent of the people who will vote for the president no matter what...who are dependent upon government, who **believe** that they are victims, who **believe** the government has a responsibility to care for them, who **believe** that they are entitled to health care, to food, to housing, to you-name-it. (Data 29)

The repetition of the same structure of **who believe that ...** can expose Romney's character that he may talk about anyone in the country and would be harsh and impertinent to those voters if he could be elected as the President of the US, whose behavior is contradictory to the western values on freedom and privacy.

It is worth mentioning here that in spite of the outstanding social status the two candidates possessed, to some extent, they were not dominating but dominated by their hearers, as they were struggling for the power rather than exerting their power. Proper use of mental processes given by the

Chapter VII Meaning-making in Verbal-Visual Interaction

candidates in positive advertising helps to create a moderate and cautious tone to display their perspectives or determination, not irritating those who don't agree with them, especially, for those potential voters. In addition, being proud of a democratic country, the speakers in positive advertising have to inform their hearers that everyone could have the same opportunity to express his/her ideas.

The most frequent occurrences in the mental processes are the words expressing their personal cognition and affection to the future of the country and the people, such as know (8 hits), want (7 hits), hope (5 hits), think (4 hits), love (3 hits), believe (2 hits). On the basis of the verbal data collected in the positive advertising, it can be noted that, Hillary Clinton, being the first female candidate for US president in history, prefers mental processes in her positive advertising to show her common beliefs, national sentiments and fortitude for the country and the people. For example:

 I **think** we can all agree it has been a long campaign.

 It is the kind of country we **want for** our children and grandchildren.

 Look, we all **know** we've come through some hard economic times and we've some pretty big changes, but I **believe in** our people.

 I **love** this country, and I **am convinced** our best days are still ahead of us if we reach for them together.

 I **want** to be a president for all Americans, not just those who support me in this election. (Data 15)

 I **believe** families deserve quality education for their kids, child care they can trust and afford, equal pay for women, and jobs they can really live on. (Data 16)

Those mental processes can help to promote listener's sympathetic reaction towards the actor in them, as different identities can be created, such as a mother, a grandmother, a patriot, a leader and a woman, encouraging the potential voters to align with her thoughts as Hillary Clinton was always being criticized to be too masculine.

Verbal processes represent the processes of saying, which are realized by direct speech or indirect speech. Though the employment of verbal processes in public discourses makes it accessible and favorable to enhance their authority and creditability in purely written or spoken forms of discourse, it should be noted that along with development of the modern technology, especially, the wide spread use of the multimedia tech help to innovate the verbal process. As a result, verbal process is not so widely used in televised political advertising, accounting for 1.19% in positive advertising and 5.34% in negative ones because of the efficiency of multimodal communication which will be elaborated later. How their words are expressed through the speaker's deliberate selection of different verbs can mirror the construction of their social power and identity. For example:

> <u>Obama</u>: For eight years, **we've been told** that the way to a stronger economy was to give huge tax breaks to corporations and the wealthiest Americans, and somehow prosperity would trickle down. (Data 3)
>
> <u>McCain</u>: **Telling** us paying higher taxes is "patriotic"? And **saying** we need to "spread the wealth around"? (Data 7)
>
> <u>John Glenn</u>: And you know he means what he says. (Data 10)

In the examples mentioned above, it can be figured out that the candidates Obama and McCain used neutral words of "have been told" "telling" and "saying" to show their negative attitudes towards the current government and its policy, implying its weakness and incompetence in managing the country as if orders or regulations made by the government have been made to be less powerful. Neither makes any judgment on it, whether it is true, exaggerated or otherwise.

Clauses with the verbs "to be" or synonyms such as "exist" "arise" or "occur" are typically existential processes which can inform the hearers that something exists or happens.

> <u>Romney (Oct. 22, 2012 debate)</u>: **There are** two very different paths the country can take. (Data 13)
>
> <u>Male Announcer</u>: **There is** a movement building in America. (Data 19)

In the invented sentences, the participant, preceded by "there be" or "there exist", may be any kind of the phenomenon and often denote a nominalized action. Comparing with the material process "The authority has negotiated with the public.", vague information on agency and responsibility can be expressed as both actor and goal can be omitted in the existential process. For example, in Romney's positive advertising, "The Clear Path", he began his debate with an existential process, denoting that two choices for the future of the country exist and implying that his audience had to make correct selections.

7.2 Meaning-making in Interpersonal Function

7.2.1 On Mood System

Fierce competition in the period of the General Campaign resulted in the increasing talk and comment about politics and some citizens become intensely involved as they get caught up by campaign advertising and mobilization (Nelson, Steven & David, 2012). Therefore, the success of a piece of political advertising largely depends on how much information and knowledge can be assimilated by its receivers. Running for the position, the candidate, on one hand, had to elaborate on their own future plans for the development of the country, such as the internal and external threats, economic policy, diplomatic strategies, etc. On the other hand, they had to attack their rivals, pointing out their deficiencies and damages in managing the countries if they could be elected. Given that facts and truths in the advertising should be presented to their voters in a neutral and rational way, the employment of declarative clauses must be the best choice for the ideological control of the public. For example:

<u>Obama:</u> Instead of prosperity trickling down, **pain** has **trickled up. Working family incomes have fallen** by two thousand dollars a year. We're losing jobs. **Deficits** are exploding. **Our economy** is in turmoil. (Obama, 2008, Data 3)

This ad was released on the day that Obama outlined his "New Energy for America Plan" in a speech in Lansing, MI. An exact and distinct description of the financial problems American people were facing could deliver the audience vivid but objective information via the employment of declarative clauses, encouraging the voters to make a change.

Statistics in Table 24 reveal that interrogative and imperative clauses are not preferred in televised political adverting for the reason that they can't meet the demand of voters in terms of interpersonal function. The imperative clause is used to realize three functions, namely, commands, requests or appeals. It should be related to the exertion of power and social status, commands or orders indicating that the social positions between the speakers and hearers are not equal.

However, in the presidential campaign, the candidates can't exercise power. Instead, they try to struggle for power, as it is commonly believed that their power is endowed by God and the people. Too many imperative clauses will make their speeches sound peremptory, opinionated and unfriendly, hindering bridging the distance between speakers and hearers. Therefore, only a few imperative clauses can be found in both positive and negative advertising.

The proper use of imperative clauses can produce special communicative effects in certain social and linguistic contexts. The following examples are selected from the collection of positive advertising:

McCain (voiceover): **Do hope for** a stronger America! **Vote** for one. **Join** me. (Data 5)

McCain: **Stand up with** me! **Let's fight for** America. (Data 26)

Clinton: Tomorrow **let's** make history together. (Data 15)

In the first example, John McCain asks for the voters' support. Though his expression is direct and tough, he tries to establish the voters' confidence on him and the future of the country by using imperative clause in an emphatic structure first. The expression of "Let's" in an imperative clause is common in public discourses with the purpose of making an appeal to the audience to take an action. In the second and third examples, Both John McCain and Hillary Clinton called on their voters to work together with them for the country, which sounds encouraging and inspiring by intriguing their patriotism. Moreover, it helps to establish the candidates' prestige and

Chapter VII Meaning-making in Verbal-Visual Interaction

authority as the most powerful leader of the country.

Interrogative clauses basically function as questions or interrogations. But the functions of interrogative clauses have been extended and treated as an important tool in argumentation as it will make the hearers feel involved in the events discussed in the advertising. Sometimes the speaker's words will appear in the question-and-answer form with the aim of arousing the hearer's interests, emphasizing some general knowledge, attitudes, and points of view, etc. and making a deep impression on the hearers. For example:

> Obama: At this defining moment in our history, the question is not, **"are you better off than you were four years ago?"** We all know the answer to that. The real question is **"will our country be** better off four years from now"? **How will we** lift our economy and restore America's place in the world? (Data 2)

Obama begins his advertising with question-and-answer form with the purpose of encouraging the audience to be involved in his talk to raise two more questions about the economic development and the position of the country in the world, which should be given more attention. As a matter of fact, no exact answers from the audience are demanded by Obama. Instead, the speaker himself has his own answers to those two questions that will be elaborated on later. The main purpose of using interrogative clauses here is to draw their curiosity andattention.

Comparatively, the distribution of interrogative clauses in negative advertising similar to that in positive ones for the reason that the same strategy can be applied for the sake of arising the voters' concentration on the defects in the main characters' personalities and policies, resulting in some negative feelings upon the characters in the advertising. For example:

> Obama: But the McCain tax could cost your family thousands. Can you afford it? (Data 24)
>
> Obama: How much would you pay? Romney just won't say. (Data 31)

In the first example, the interrogative clause goes after a statement that McCain's tax policy would increase household expenditure. It is clear that the speaker is waiting for a definitely negative answer from the audience, which can cause their reflection and anxiety on their future life. Similarly, in the second example, the speaker, following question-answer form, raised a special question first, then answered the question directly so as to stress that Romney dishonestly tell them the truth that his policy would do harm to their benefits.

7.2.2 On Modal Auxiliaries

Statistics in Table 24 show that all the candidates cared about their tones in both positive and negative advertising as they chose mild way of expressing their point of view because modal auxiliaries like **will, can** are milder, more modest and less objective than such modal auxiliaries like **have to, must**, indicating that their cautions and discreetness on their exertion of power. Frequent appearances of modal auxiliaries with high values are contrast to the values of freedom and democracy in western values in politics.

Statistics in Table 24 also show that more modal verbs are used in positive advertising than negative ones. In positive advertising, the modal verbs "will" with median value is most frequently used, accounting for more than 50% of the total number of modal verbs. Through the analysis of different meanings of the word "will", different implications can be delivered to the audience in different context.

Generally speaking, the modal verb "will" indicates a future event. In terms of its meanings, Concordance in Antconc shows that 40 times of the total number are used affirmatively, 4 negatively with the word "not" and 6 in questions in positive advertising for the purpose of expressing their future plans, prediction, self-evaluation, determination and proposals. For example:

  McCain: The last eight years haven't worked very well, have they? **I will** make the next four better. (Data 7)

  Romney (Oct. 22, 2012 debate): **I will** work with you. **I will** lead you in an open and honest way. (Data 13)

Chapter Ⅶ Meaning-making in Verbal-Visual Interaction

   Clinton: **I will** work my heart out as president to make life better for you and your family. (Data 15)
   Romney (Oct. 22, 2012 debate): The President's path **will** mean continuing declining in take-home pay. (Data 13)
   Clinton: I hope you **will** think about. (Data 15)

The common characteristic in the first three examples is that the word "will" is used to express their own beliefs, promises, thought and wishes as the leader of the nation and then concrete policies are given to the voters. In spite of the great difficulties in the current situation, their confidence on their leadership has been delivered. Mild suggestions also have been made to the voters with the help of the word "will" in Clinton's words, indicating a future action taken by the potential voters.

The word "will" only appears 19 times in negative advertising, 9 of which are used in negative sentences, showing the speakers' negative judgment and opinions towards their opponents' dishonesty and disabilities in leading the country as demonstrated in the following examples.

   Obama: And since McCain **will not** require coverage for pre-existing conditions, finding a new plan could leave you hanging by a thread. (Data 23)
   Obama: But here is what he **will not** tell you. (Data 24)
   Obama: He **will not** reveal what is in his taxes. (Data 31)

Apart from "will", in positive advertising, the occurrences of the word "can" ranks second, which is an important indicator of competence and probability of the whole clause. "Can" is frequently used in the affirmative clause in the campaign advertising with the purpose of self-praise and self-promotion. For example:

   Obama: Because if we stand together, we **can** meet our challenges and ensure that there are better days ahead. (Data 2)
   Obama: I know that we **can** steer ourselves out of this crisis. (Data 3)
   Obama: we **can** keep moving America forward. (Data 11)
   Clinton: we face big challenges but we **can** solve them the same way families do. (Data 18)

Concordance shows that 65% of its usage appearing in the same sentence structure "*we can do*" in the positive advertising implies that great benefits can be brought towards the American people if the candidates can be selected. It is an important implication that all the candidates themselves in the positive advertising tried to tell the voters that they were more competent and confident for the American president if those voters can align with them. In addition, the simple sentences are more legible, rhythmical and arresting in terms of their phonological features.

On the contrary, the word "can" is less frequently used in negative advertising. However, Along with the word "not" in negative televised political advertising, its usage indicates disability and the impossibility that all the citizens have rights and ability to make correct choices, avoiding any possibility that their opponents do harm to them or the incompetence of their opponents in leading the nation. Concordance proves that 4 of 5 times in negative advertising are used in such a context. For example:

Romney: Five reasons we **can not** afford four more years of Barack Obama. (Data 32)

Trump: I **can not** say that either.

Trump (clip): You **can not** lead this nation if you have such a low opinion for its citizens.

Among the modal auxiliaries with high value, the modal auxiliary "have got to" is employed most frequently because it is more objective than the other two ones, emphasizing the necessity and obligation both the candidates themselves and the voters should be faced with. For example:

Romney: And for that to happen, we're going to **have to** have a president who can work across the aisle. (Data 13)

Romney: Next, you **have got to** balance the budget. You **have got to** cut the deficit. You **have got to** stop spending more money than we take in. (Data 14)

Obama: To pay for huge new tax breaks for millionaires like him, Romney **would have to** raise taxes on the middle class. (Data 31)

In the first example, Romney emphasized the emergency and necessity of selecting a president who can make a balanced budget and urged the voters to make a correct selection by using the phrase "have to", which helped him

Chapter VII Meaning-making in Verbal-Visual Interaction

to enhance his obligation, confidence and ability to lead the country by guaranteeing his potential voters a better economic life, establishing favorable relationship with his voters. In the second example, the use of "have got to" in a sequence implies his great power and confidence in his future policy as a presidential candidate. The fourth example extracts from Obama's attack against Romney, answering the question Mitt Romney and Paul Ryan won't: how to pay for their $5 trillion tax cuts skewed to millionaires and billionaires. The use of "have to" with a subjective mood indicates his objective evaluation on the bad consequences of his rival's policy towards the middle class, highlighting his precipitance and incompetence of being a leader.

7.2.3 On Personal Pronouns

It can be inferred from Table 25 that the singular forms of first-person pronouns are most frequently employed, especially "I" reaching 178 times consisting of 103 in positive advertising and 75 in negative advertising respectively, for several reasons:

Firstly, for each piece of televised campaign advertising, there are two simple clauses ritually delivered to the audience at the beginning or at the end of each piece for the self-introduction to advertiser and the approval of his/her promise towards the authenticity of the message in the ad, like "**I** am Donald Trump, and **I** approved the message." in his running for the presidency in 2016. Therefore, among 178 times of its representations in 42 pieces of campaign advertising, nearly 50% of the total number is used in such a context. It can be considered as the construction of overwhelming dominance and power in discourses because not everyone can have access to campaign advertising, the repetitive appearance of the first person "I" in a parallel structure aiming to highlight their eminent fame and position as presidential candidates and consolidate their image and identity in the voters' mind.

Secondly, the first person pronoun "I" can also be used to clarify one's opinion, belief, plan and obligation in a mild way in political struggles. In campaign advertising, not imposing their ideology upon all the voters, it is safe for the candidates to choose "I" when talking about their future plans just because it is impossible for everyone to agree with them, which makes their words sound responsible, modest, prudent and reasonable. For example:

<u>McCain</u>: I will reform Wall Street and fix Washington. **I** have taken on tougher guys than this before. (Data 8)

<u>Clinton (to camera)</u>: **I** will get up every day determined to keep America safe and strong and make our economy work for everyone, not just those at the top. **I** will work my heart out as president to make life better for you and your family. (Data 15)

Both McCain and Clinton in the two examples show their own ability, responsibility and determination to work hard as the American President to arouse the voters' affirmative feelings and sympathetic responses and then appeal for their support and approval.

Statistics in Table 25 indicate that the plural forms of the first-person pronoun are preferred in positive advertising whichis consistent with the finding that the inclusive pronouns like we, us, our are regarded as the most powerful political and ideological pronouns for political discourse in general, implying that the speaker and his/her listeners shares the common interests (Wilson 1990). In the political discourses, proper use of those pronouns can shorten the social distance between people from different social ranks. Humble or noble, everyone is treated equally here. It will make them firmly believe that they, both the speakers and the hearers, are on the same foot. For example:

<u>Obama</u>: Because if **we** stand together, **we** can meet **our** challenges and ensure that there are better days ahead. (Data 2)

<u>Obama</u>: **we** are not there yet but **we** have made real progress and the last thing **we** should do is to turn back now. (Data 11)

<u>Trump</u>: This is **our** country. **We** can change directions and make America great again. (Data 19)

In those three examples, all the speakers, as the leader of nation, tried

Chapter Ⅶ Meaning-making in Verbal-Visual Interaction

to speak for the audience, aiming to emphasize the common challenges they had to face with, the progresses they had made and the common benefits and values they had stick to through the deliberate selection of the plural forms of the first person pronouns in a sequence. Those encouraging and eloquent words help to establish an intimate relationship between the candidates and the voters, and thus to convince them to join and support them in the election.

Oppositely, in negative advertising, the plural forms of the first-person pronoun are least frequently used because the ultimate purpose of making those advertising is to alienate their opponents from potential voters by exposing their weaknesses in an objective way. Therefore, in the fewer examples in negative advertising, the use of the word "We" aims to distinguish their opponents with the advertisers and the voters. For example:

>   Announcer: **We** are going to have an international crisis to test the mettle of **this guy.** (Data 26)
>   Announcer: Five reasons **we** can not afford four more years of **Barack Obama.** (Data 32)
>   Romnney: Under **Obama**, **we**'ve lost over half a million manufacturing jobs. (Data 34)

The common feature in those examples is that the speakers pointed out the crisis and the loss they would have to undertake if their opponents could be selected, highlighting their concern for the future of the country and the people and the incompetence and indifference of their opponents towards the common interests they demanded. On one hand, They tried to separate their rivals from all the other Americans including themselves so as to emphasize the duty of being the leader of the US; on the other hand, it seems that they were representatives of all Americans who were speaking for them with the aim of pointing out the serious mistakes that their rivalsmight made in their plans which is well-known as rhetorical ploy of populist democracy. It can help to remind the voters of reflecting on their future and making correct decisions. It is clear that the inclusive pronouns referring to the first-person pronouns such as *we*, *us*, *our* can show great solidarity, indicating the support for each other or for the intra group, especially in political or international affairs.

Comparatively, the application of second-person pronouns shows the reduction of solidarity or the fortificationof power. Statistics indicate that other kinds of exclusive pronouns also occur in both positive and negative advertising; its implied meanings in different context are vary.

7.3 Meaning-making in Interactive Function

7.3.1 On Contact

The fundamental function of advertising is to supply the viewers with necessary and expected information. With necessary elaboration and explanation, certain kinds of interaction, such as warning, appealing, request, command and etc. can naturally be made between the elements in the advertising and the viewers. For this sake, the receivers are presumed to be observers or onlookers, receiving the information in a passive way. They can have their own recognition and judgment based on the common cognition on the facts but no feedback is needed. On one hand, the advertisers have to inform the voters their future blueprints, personalities and leadership built on positive advertising as qualified leaders of the nation. In the negative advertising, on the other hand, the disastrous consequences in the rivals' future policies, their physical and psychological weaknesses can be vividly and impressively exposed to the viewers in the images. To provide an overview of the results on the function of offer image, the following is the typical visual data gathered from the corpus:

Chapter VII Meaning-making in Verbal-Visual Interaction

Figure 21   Something

Figure 21 is a typical example including nine pieces of "offer images", illustrating the popularity and leadership of Barack Obama as the presidential candidate in his campaign activities. Both Obama and his supporters have no eye contact with the viewers. However, certain kinds of social relations through eye contacts and gestures inside the images between Obama and his supporters can still be perceived by the viewers. In those pictures, a hardworking, amiable, respected and powerful image of a presidential candidate has been objectively constructed with the help of other gestures, such as big smiles, his handshaking with the electors, the applauses and Obama's highly raising hand in his speeches. The representations in the images can produce appealing and impressive effect, attracting more potential voters to support him.

Rebuilding the American dream 1

Rebuilding the American dream 2

Rebuilding the American dream 3

Rebuilding the American dream 4

Rebuilding the American dream 5

Rebuilding the American dream 6

Rebuilding the American dream 7

Rebuilding the American dream 8

Rebuilding the American dream 9

Figure 22　Rebuilding the American Dream

According to visual grammar, images in Figure 22 belong to analytical processes relating participants in terms of a part-whole structure, describing Trump's blueprint of improving the American economic situation from different aspects. In one analytical picture, there is no vector or tree structure and "It serves to identify a carrier and to allow viewers to scrutinize this carrier's Possessive Attributes." (Kress and Van Leeuwen, 2006). No human beings appear and no eye contact occurs in those analytical processes. Thus, images without human or quasi-human participants looking directly at the viewer are of "offer image" in which no contact takes place. The analytical process appears commonly in political discourses, in the forms of kinds of statistic graphs, procedures and deconstruction of objects, etc. Integrating with language, it can provide the viewers information of scientific, straight, precise, concrete and objective values. Trump's concepts of rebuilding the American dreams covering every aspect of social life in those pictures, the symbolic meanings of the high-rise skyscrapers in Image 1, rotating numbers in Image 3 and the completion of the national map from Image 6 to Image 7 give the viewers deep and vivid impression.

Chapter VII Meaning-making in Verbal-Visual Interaction

However, "offer images" in negative advertising may lead to different effects. It can be noted that Romney in Figure 11 avoids his direct eye contact with the viewers by slightly looking downwards (Image 1-3) or upwards (Image 8-9) with different meaning potentials. His slightly downward sight indicates his disability and distrust; while his slightly upward sight reveals his arrogance and self-conceit. Comparatively, Image 7 with an old couple looking at the fame is a typical "demand image" in which they try to invite the viewers to answer the question "How much would you pay?" Naturally, it can raise the viewers' empathy and doubt on Romney's Tax Policy.

Figure 23 Won't Say

Statistics in Table 27 indicate that more "demand image" occur in positive advertising than in negative ones. Among 55 pieces of "demand images" in positive campaign advertising, it can be noted that 42 of them are given by the candidates and the rest are given by their supporters and political allies in the form of their direct looking at the camera while talking about their opinions, plans and determination, etc. for the reason that they want to get the reactors" consensus. In Figure 24, Obama talks about his plans without any detachment of his sights from the camera. Neutral emotions could be perceived by the reactors through his eye contact with them because he needs their recognition on his identity of a decisive leader, their sober reflection on his speech and their affirmative feedback towards his plans.

Figure 24　Defining Moment

　　The distinctive feature in Figure 25 is that Hillary Clinton's direct gazes accompanied with her changes of facial expressions. This piece of advertising known as her personal and positive closing message, her smiles from a front angle can help to shorten the social distance with the voters and encourage them to stand with her and vote for her.

The same strategy was used by Hillary Clinton in her positive advertising entitled "Tomorrow".

Figure 25 Tomorrow

Comparatively, the analysis of 26 pieces of "demand images" in negative advertising reveals that the possible reactions are expected while such characters as the candidates of the other Party and their victims express their negative feelings to the viewer. In Figure 26, for example, the first eight images are "demand image", as the characters with different identities in them gazed at the camera. Their noticeable dull eyes along with stiff faces transmitting their negative feelings of disappointment, helplessness, sadness and anger towards Trump's words greatly impressed the reactors, as if they would have been involved in the same plight as the characters in the advertising did and the same reactions towards Trump were demanded from them. Similar strategies can be found in Data 29, Data 31 and Data 41 as well.

Figure 26　We are America

All in all, the reactor's continuous eye contact with the viewers can help to construct certain kinds of social relations, because the viewers are considered imaginary participants involved in the events described in the advertising and demanded to choose from certain kind of reaction or response. However, as it is indicated before, in the reaction process the reactors have to make two options: the option of phenomenon and the option of directions. Instead of direct eye contact with the viewers, characters in the image can choose to look upwards, downwards, leftwards and rightwards or they can simply close their eyes; they can look at any object in the image as the phenomenon or they can look off frame aimlessly. Obviously, the intentional choices made by the producer have become a meaning potential, revealing great implicit meaning. It should be noted that being strongly cultural-specific and contextual-specific, gazes may have different "metaphorical implications" (Machin, 2012). Its interpretation should be correlated to other kinds of body language and the existing circumstances.

7.3.2 On Size of Frame

Proper portion of details revealed in medium shots can enhance its objectivity, authenticity, reliability and thus its force of persuasion, establishing certain kinds of social relations between the participants and the viewers. On the contrary, close-up shots are more suitable for expressing both positive and negative emotions because certain characteristics of the participants in the images can be exemplified and more impressive and attractive to the viewers. Thus, certain kinds of close relations or attitudes, either hostile or intimate ones, can be constructed between the participants in the image and the viewers. The result can be demonstrated in the following examples:

Figure 27　Same Path

Figure 27 shows a dynamic change of lens from medium to extreme close-up shots, suggesting that two kinds of interpersonal relations have been established. For the most part of his elaboration on the current economic problems and his distinctive ideas on the future economic plan from McCain's, medium shots have been adopted because his reactors' attention will not be distracted from the images but be paid to his speech. In addition, proper social distance between Obama and his viewers demonstrated in medium shot can establish his identity of being the presidential candidate, showing his dominate power and leadership to his viewers. However, approaching to his smiling faces in extreme close-up shots at the end gives the viewers an impression that they have been involved in his speech, which helps to establish an intimate relationship between them. the viewers are likely to be moved by his words as well as his confidence and charisma with the distance gradually shortened.

Figure 28   Tiny

It is indicated before, that the main participants in negative advertising are the candidates of the other side, their victims and opponents. Therefore,

Chapter Ⅶ Meaning-making in Verbal-Visual Interaction

too many close-up shots in negative advertising will make the candidates extremely individual, subjective and aggressive as all the viewers' attention will be attracted to their unfriendly facial expressions, such as arrogance, anger, harshness, hopelessness and etc., which can produce alienation effect to the viewers. In addition, close look at the victims' facial expressions in negative advertising will lead to the viewers' sympathy towards those victims as well as hatred and distrust towards the candidates. The following example comes from Romney's attack against Obama's diplomatic policy in the Middle East:

A sharp contrast between the close-up shots of Obama's expressions of his aloofness and graveness and medium shots on the nuclear threats and terrorism emphasizes his incapability in dealing with those serious problems.

The maximum of information can be distinctly uncovered in the selection of long shot which can construct public distance within which participants inside and outside of the images remain strangers. Another most outstanding feature of long shot is that no focus can be noticed by the viewers which can enhance the sense of unfamiliarity.

Apart from the construction of relations between the participants and the viewers, the interpersonal relations among the participants inside the image can be exposed inside. Generally speaking, the change of lens will determine how many participants will be involved in an image; the longer the lens is, the more people will be involved and the more details will be unveiled. In the other words, the producers' selection of "size of frame" is relevant to the choice of collectivism and individualism in a certain context. Through analysis of the images in both positive advertising, it can be noticed that candidates themselves are usually include in an intra-group in medium or long shots to show their interactions with their voters or they are in a out-group in close-up shots to highlight their dominant power. A balance between the solidarity and power has been kept for the candidates with the Americans in positive advertising. However, seldom are the candidates from the other party depicted as a member of a group; they remain isolated and alienated from the public.

7.3.3 On Perspective

The horizontal angle is related to the involvement or detachment between the image-producers and the represented participants (Kress and Van Leeuwen, 2006). According to Ravelli (2008), while the frontal angle is relevant to "the subjective engagement with the image; the oblique angle reflects detachment with the image". It seems that participants seen from the frontal angel trying to invite the viewers to have a face-to-face interaction with them, which can shorten the social distance between the participants and their viewers. On the other hand, the oblique angles encourage the viewers to appreciate an image from an side-on view, giving them the most naturalistic, authentic and objective views of the events depicted in the image.

Figure 29 comes from Hillary Clinton's positive advertising, highlighting Hillary Clinton's devotion to working for children and families as the leader of the nation. Frontal angles in the seven images except Image 2 and Image 8 give the viewers a deep sense of involvement that they are invited to be engaged in experiencing their children's growth and appreciating every happy moment of family life depicted in the image as if they were members of the family. In the second and eighth image, medium shots from the oblique angle can create scenes of real family life indicate that the viewers are close observer of the scenes. Though they are detached from the events happening in the image, they are still encouraged to align with their happiness. All the images give the viewers a deep impression that what Clinton will do is beneficial for every US citizen including the viewers themselves, which can help her to win over the favors from the average Americans.

Chapter VII Meaning-making in Verbal-Visual Interaction

Figure 29 Measure

On the other hand, more oblique angles than frontal ones are chosen in negative ones. More detachments instead of involvements have been chosen because the image producers encourage the viewers to hold an objective perspective towards the uncovered or unnoticed events described in the images and deliberately enlarge the social distance between the represented participants from the viewers with an implication that the miseries and difficulties could be avoided if they have held a chance to make a good choice. For example:

Figure 30 entitled as **Dangerous** is Trump's attack against Clinton. Confronted with the threat and expansion of terrorism depicted in the first four pictures, the accurate and detailed exposure of Clinton's weaknesses and indifference in Image 6, Image 7 and Image 8, such as her constant coughs, staggering steps and etc. can arouse the voters' curiosity and doubt on the deep-rooted cognition of strong image possessed by American President. The secret but authentic information unmasked from the oblique angles can persuade the viewers to make a rational judgment that Hillary's selection to be the President could be a great danger towards their safety. By contrast, frontal angles transmit negative emotions to the viewers. Hillary Clinton wearing a pair of sunglasses in the conference room, her indulgence in her cell phones indicates that dishonest, the viewers are involved in guessing and pursuing the truth concealed by her.

Figure 30　Dangerous

As a result, Strong sense of involvement can be achieved by the choice of frontal angel, as if both the image-producers and the viewers, sharing the same points of view, should belong to certain groups of represented participants. On the contrary, the oblique angle can deliver a sense of detachment since it implies that the image-producersdon't belong to any group of represented participants depicted in the image.

As for the vertical angle, it "transmits power relationship between the represented participants and the viewers and between the represented participants within an image" (Guijarro & Sanz, 2008). There are three choices: high-angle, low-angle, and eye-level angle. In a high-angle picture, the represented participants are seen from a higher position, which makes them look small or weak or vulnerable while a low-angle picture is seen from below the represented participants, making them look powerful, authoritative or

Chapter VII Meaning-making in Verbal-Visual Interaction

threatening. The choice of eye-level angle has little psychological effect on the viewer, manifesting an equal and harmonious relationship between the represented participants and the viewers.

Thorough examinations on the distribution of vertical angles in both positive and negative advertising indicate that more preferences are given to eye-level angles than to high-angle and low angle pictures. In positive ad, the eye-leveled pictures help to shorten the social distance between the candidates and the viewers for the reason that equal relations are constructed. In addition, both positive and negative advertising with their main purpose of persuading, the viewers need to have a naturalistic angle to appreciate the pictures. Therefore, their selections of eye-leveled pictures can enhance their objectivity.

It should be emphasized that the selection of perspective is made not by the represented participants or the viewers but by the image-producers. As the selection of different perspectives and angels in the image construction can mirror the change of social relations and the distribution of power in the political discourses, its study can faithfully unmask the image-producer's implicit attitude, ideology and interests.

7.3.4 On Modality Markers

Naturalistic colors capable of reflecting certainty and reality existing in the real world are endowed with high modality whose implied meaning is similar to the modal auxiliaries like **must, have to and will** in terms of their interpersonal meaning. The main participants in positive advertising are the advertisers, their supporters and beneficiaries; it is likely for them to be engaged in the advertising by themselves. As the priority for meaning-making should be given to the persuasive force on their performance in the advertising, their participation in form of talk show or in various activities is treated to be more reliable and realistic because the authentic portrayal in color friendly to the eyes can greatly shorten the distance between participants and viewers. Furthermore, its neutrality encourages viewers to focus on their speeches so that they can make a rational and correct decision.

All the shots selected by the producers are taken in daily life without any artistic modification. Naturalistic colors, such as the recognizable color saturation of hair, clothing, skin, environment and etc, indicate that those images are the real mirror of family life as well as the true delineation of Hillary's special concern and care for the welfare of the younger generation. Strong senses of vividness and credibility make those images more convincing and impressive.

Figure 31 Families First

On the other hand, non-naturalistic colors go to two extremes: natural colors are partially weakened or completely lost in an image or color saturations may be exaggerated in it. Given this, non-naturalistic colors fail to reflect the truth of the physical world. Hence, its usage suggests subjectivity, uncertainty, impossibility and imagination. The outstanding advantage of employing non-naturalistic colors in communication is that its artificial and artisticexpression can be a reliable reflection of the producers' emotions. Since naturalistic colors are regarded as watershed of neutral feelings, emotions are intensified or weakened along with the changing degrees of color saturation. For the purpose of expressing negative emotions,

Chapter VII Meaning-making in Verbal-Visual Interaction

such as, dissatisfaction towards the candidates of the other party, terror of the crisis, fear of the victims, more weakened color saturations appear in negative advertising. Though simplicity can be expressed, comparatively negative attitudes, such as nostalgia, terror, uncertainty, monotony and the like reach to the utmost. For example, fading colors in in Figure 32 result in great difficulty in the identification of the details. Therefore, low modality can be revealed in those images. On one hand, slogans appearing in black and white are highlighted for their sharp contrast. On the other hand, the viewers can be infected by the negative emotions of anxiety, uncertainty and distrust towards Romney's policy.

Figure 32 Decision

The exaggeration of naturalistic color results in the intensified emotions for the purpose of emphasizing vivid, impressive and salient features. It often appears in the cartoons, films and advertising, aiming to highlight certain characteristics of the represented participants. For example, in the Obama's negative advertising named *Unravel* against McCain, the distinctive red color, in contrast to dominant hues of black and white, is used to highlight the salient features of a tangled thread, metaphorically implying that its intricacy can't be settled by McCain. Apparently, its truth value has been lowered, but the persuasive force can be fortified because of the eye-catching color.

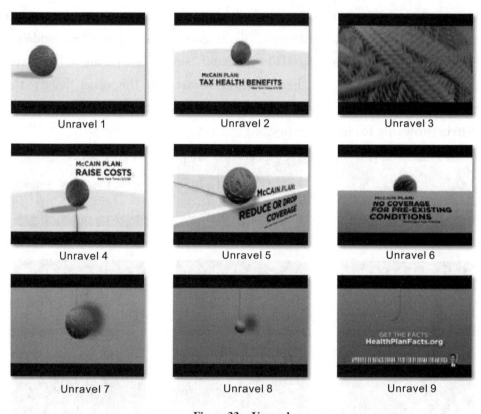

Figure 33 Unravel

A thorough analysis of the samples in positive advertising suggests that images positioned in naturalistic contexts can give the viewers a paramount view. For the positive self-representations, the candidates are often placed in specific contexts for two reasons: Firstly, its authenticity and reliability can be enhanced, as more details about their engagement with the voters and devotions to the country are provided in the image. Secondly, the balance of foregrounding and background in naturalistic view facilitates their building of power relations with other participants; their identity as strong leaders who care for the people can be shown to the viewers. Randy Henry, a coal

Chapter Ⅶ Meaning-making in Verbal-Visual Interaction

miner and supporter of Obama, talks about Obama's contribution to saving the coal industry in Southern Illinois in Figure 34. It can be noted that eight images except Image 5 employ a naturalistic context, in which the specifications on the speaker" activities and Obama's interaction with the local people. Though no salience can be distinguished by the viewers, the equal importance given to the participants and the environment impresses the viewers with Obama's intimate relations with the American people. In addition, specific description of the background information in full contextualization with high values reaffirms Obama's contributions.

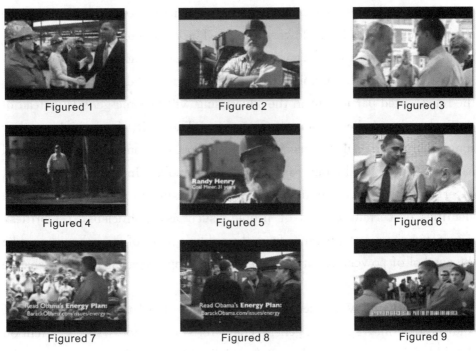

Figure 34 Figure

7.3.5 On Contextualization

Enlightened by the Malinowski's anthropological semantics in the study of context in meaning, the London school with Firth (1930) and Halliday (1978) as the representatives, proposed and developed the concept of contextualism, referring to the context situation in which language is used.

Similarly, two layers of images can be recognized by viewers: foregrounding and background. Foregrounding refers to the most approachable and salient part in an image to the viewers. Background in visual modes refers to contexts that the foregrounding is involved in. Therefore, the more blurred the background is, the more salient the foregrounding becomes. For the communicative purpose, the amount of background information exposed to the viewers depends on the degrees of the contextualization, consisting of naturalistic, blurred and absent contexts, all of which were found and calculated as shown in Table 27.

Along with the increasing degrees of blurred contextualization, the truth values are gradually lowered down. The complete absence of context results in the lowest modality, indicating vagueness and uncertainty. By de-contextualization, the prominent features of foregrounding are highlighted; the represented participant in the advertising will become generic instead of particular, symbolic rather than specific. The shift from high to low contextualization can be regarded as a process from the concrete and narrative to the abstract as well as symbolic. In televised political advertising, the de-contextualized image mainly aims to reveal the distinctive identities of certain groups of people, such as, politicians, celebrities, terrorists, victims etc. because from the public's point of view they should be the symbol of power, beauty, terror or sufferings regardless of the change of settings.

As Kress and Van Leeuwen (2006) argue that "the emotive value of color is sometimes seen as a general characteristic of color", special attention should be given to the complexity of modality markers. The evaluation on the degrees of modality is somewhat instinctive, unreliable and subjective, since human cognition and definition towards nature and reality vary with the individual's physical and psychological state. However, it is the cognitive discrepancy and limitation that make it possible that social relation can be constructed through modality, as the image-producers can align or alienate themselves with the viewers and the represented participants through the distortion of the viewer's recognition of the real world. Therefore, the image-producer's communicative intention should be related to the study of modality markers, because it is dominant and pre-determined to the design. In addition, the comprehensive analysis of modality is needed, as the absence of any modality markers, the moderate exposure of the details, the metaphorical portray of the distinctive features and the painting of hyper-reality can reflect the image-maker's kinds of attitudes or opinions towards the naturalistic existence.

7.4 Interaction Between Verbal and Visual Modes

Fariclough (1995) proposes that the innovation in multimedia technology over traditional printed media lies in its extension from "frozen modality of newspaper photographs to the movement and action in television". In the real practice of communication, the delivery of certain meaning may be presented in a certain form or the combination of different forms with the same meaning in the communication (Kress & Van Leeuwen, 2001). For a certain purpose of social interaction, namely, "deletion, addition, substitution and evaluation" (Machin, 2013), the use of the language can't be fixed in linguistic forms only but needs to be extended to the collaboration with other multimodal resources. Rough analysis of televised political advertising suggests that multimodality is the fundamental characteristic that both verbal and visual modes are combined as the coherent unity of meaning potentials, realizing three meta-functions in discourse.

Influenced by Barthe's definitions of "anchorage" and "relay", Kress (2005) distinguishes "elaboration" from "extension" in his proposal of verbal-visual relations. In terms of the communicative effects, the third question will focus on the interaction of both visual and verbal modes from the perspective of two aspects.

Elaboration in verbal-visual relations refers to consistency in meaning-making within texts and images, as Kress (2005) claims that certain words are selected to match with the possible meanings implied in the images. Details provided in one mode are obviously relevant to those supplied in the other mode, the logical relationship of specification belonging to this kind. Without texts, people from different backgrounds can have different interpretation towards images. Similarly, lack of necessary illustrations of images makes a text abstract and implausible. Therefore, proper elaboration can limit the meaning of images or languages in a certain scale, achieving certain kinds of communicative effects.

Kress (2005) proposes that two modes of verbal and visual ones send "different but semantically related information". While Elaboration refers to the interaction between visual-verbal modes within the image; extension focuses on their collaboration beyond the image. If elaboration is regarded as a kind of overt relations in meaning-making, in other words, the logic relations between visual and verbal modes in extension need the viewer's recognition and classification for the reason that though logically related, there are no direct connections and indexes between texts and images in terms of lexical meanings in the texts and denoted entities in the pictures.

Provided that the corresponding functional categorization in SFG and VG has been made by Kress (1996), two aspects of interaction between verbal and visual modes will be discussed on the basis of the previous analysis: one is elaboration on ideational meaning and the other is extension on interpersonal meaning.

7.4.1 Elaboration on Ideational Meaning

What in language is realized by words of the category "action verbs" or processes in ideational meaning is visually realized by elements that can be formally defined as "vectors". The "actor" is the participant from whom or which the vector departs, and which may be fused with the vector to different degrees (Kress and Van Leeuwen, 2006). By relating the actions in images to the verbs in text, ideational elaboration can be divided into elaborations on references, events and concepts.

7.4.2 Elaboration on References

Referenced Elaboration refers to the specific explanation on the resources of texts in communication. It commonly appears in a verbal process or a mental process through the verbs "to say" "to think" "to know" "to feel" and its many synonyms. The employment of verbal or mental processes in the public discourses may enhance their authority and creditability, as it is commonly believed that words originated from definite resources are more reliable, persuasive and powerful to the hearers. However, the analysis of ideational processes indicates that verbal and mental processes are not preferable in televised political advertising. The fundamental reason is that verbal or mental processes in televised political advertising requires specification of their speakers or addressers and surroundings in which interactions take place under the multimodal contexts.

Verbal or mental process, equivalent to projective process in linguistic system, must be processes of mixing both linguistic forms and visual forms. "The oblique protrusions of dialogue balloons" can connect "drawings of speakers to their speech" (Kress & Van Leeuwen, 2006). In verbal, participants in a verbal process from whom the "dialogue balloon" emanates are known as speakers or sensors. Along with the development of modern technology, especially, the wide spread use of the multimedia tech help to innovate the verbal processes. Though no dialogue balloon appears on the screen, the face-to-face interviews, public speech, talk shows and etc launched by the Sayers which are broadcasted on TV can also be regarded as verbal processes, words in which can be transformed into texts. To some extent, the mechanism of the verbal process in visual grammar is quite similar to the direct speech in SFG. Therefore, it should be stressed that the words in the dialogue balloon, or the transcript from the sound system should be recognized as other processes. As long as the sayer speaks on the screen, his actions of speaking or thinking can be treated as the verbal or mental process. Along with the verbal process appearing in the image (Figure 35, Image 5), the male announcer used an indirect quotation,

"Obama says Iran is a 'tiny' country, doesn't pose a serious threat." The specification of Obama's image together with the repetition of the key words aims to establish direct connection between the speaker and the text. The multimodal design makes his idea sound more indiscreet and imprudent, arousing the viewers' dissatisfaction and anxiety.

Figure 35　Tiny Image 5

The biggest advantage in referenced elaboration in televised political advertising over traditional verbal process is that multimodal presentations in the forms of TV live or video clips can provide the viewers the most reliable data resources and give them the deepest impression through stimulating their visual as well as auditive sensory at the same time. No doubt that direct perception of the speakers' image and performance on the stage as well as their noticeable voice is more impressive, authentic, memorable and reliable than quotations in pure linguistic forms. The following example comes from Hillary's attack against Trump whose words are described to be rude, impolite, dishonest and insulting to so-called vulnerable groups, especially females and the unemployed. A series of video clips related to Trump are selected and combined to enhance its communicative effects. Meanwhile, all his words appear in the form of verbal processes. Specifications of the different environments in which his speeches took place can confirm his "low" opinion towards Americans. By relating the text with images, it can be noted that Trump's poor image is constructed, exaggerated and reinforced through the combination of different modes.

Chapter VII Meaning-making in Verbal-Visual Interaction

Figure 36 Low Opinion

Referring to texts, its resources are not only human beings but also other kinds of media, such as news television, papers, books, pamphlets, etc. For example, in Obama's positive advertising entitled **Determination**, a book named **A Plan For Job** appears in the image along with Obama's elaboration on the gist of the book. It can be noted that information with reliable resources may encourage the viewers to read his plan. Accompanying with the image, Obama asked the viewers to read his plan and make a correct decision.

Figure 37 Determination Image 8

7.4.3 Elaboration on Event

Accompanying with the events or situations discussed in off-screen voice, images related to them can be regarded as necessary examples, explanations, illustrations and emphasis on the events. Therefore, the visualization and concreteness of the material processes in the form of multimodality can arouse the viewers' attraction, facilitate their understanding and consolidate their memory. Accordingly, words inside and outside the image can also be regarded as significant connection, bridging the meaning implied in the image and the viewers' cognition. Moreover, it can constrain the viewer's attention on a certain scale. In other words, without linguistic mode, the picture is not informative and precise enough with the loss of its effectiveness because words are more plausible and accessible to the audience, while without the assistance of non-linguistic mode, it is not effective enough with the loss of its efficiency because pictures are more perceptible and attractive to the observers. In the following examples (Figure 38) a mother talks about Trump's children care plan. At the beginning of the advertising, she talked about her affection to her child and her difficulties by using such abstract words as "love, hard, stuck". Apparently, without verbal explanations, the viewer can't understand her real intentions and her relationship with the little girl. Without the images, meanwhile, it can't be imaged how deep she loves her daughter and how difficult her life is as a mother. Therefore, Images 1-4 give the viewers vivid specifications of the text talked by the lady. The movement from medium shot to close-shot can be perceived by the viewer. The big smiles on her faces and her gaze on her daughter in a bright atmosphere concretize her fondness and happiness; vivid illustration in the images can produce a convincing and impressive effect. During her talking about her difficulties, similarly, the selection of dark atmosphere and her unhappy faces exemplify the difficulties childcare has brought to her.

Chapter Ⅶ Meaning-making in Verbal-Visual Interaction

Figure 38   Listening

The next example comes from Obama's positive advertising entitled **Determination**. In his elaboration on the achievement he has made during the past four years, corresponding images appear on the screen. The first image in figure 39 is taken from a long shot, a man running without stop. Without the text, the viewers can't understand what has happened in it. Therefore, Obama gives us a corresponding explanation of its metaphorical meaning that "there is **no quit** in America". Taken from the frontal angle, the next image shows that a woman is carefully reading a material in her office. Great implications have been sent to the viewers that they are encouraged to be engaged in reading the material with the woman. Verbally, Obama said that "you are **seeing that** right now". Another metaphorical meaning can be perceived. His visualized words can possibly arouse the audience's attention and curiosity. In addition, a hug to the daughter given by an American soldier concretizes his words that **And our heroes are coming home**. Obama tells the audience that his policies are correct and effective, and he has made some achievements and progresses during his term of office through the specification.

Figure 39　Determination

7.4.4　Elaboration on Concepts

Corresponding to existential and relational processes in linguistic forms, a concept is comparatively abstract, static and symbolic so as to express the meaning of existence, possessions or sequence. For example, apart from the freeze frame of Obama's representation in Image 9, Figure 39, the English word **Forward** containing a special design of the letter "O" painted as an icon of American flag is attractive to the viewers as well. Apparently, the conceptual meaning of the image should be related to the implied meaning of the word. The capital letter "O" means Obama himself because "O" is the initial letter in his name. In addition, this letter also belongs to part of the word "forward", expressing a concept that choosing Obama as the leader means great improvement and progress. Therefore, relevant study to the text can unfold the real meaning of a sign.

A symbol is taken into consideration, which focuses on what a participant means or is. It represents the participants as being representative of or standing for something else. Van Leeuwen and Kress (2006) divide

Chapter Ⅶ Meaning-making in Verbal-Visual Interaction

symbolic processes into symbolic attributive and symbolic suggestive processes. Symbolic attributive process has more than one participant. The meaning or identity of the main participant or carrier is determined in relation to those of the other participants, functioning as attributes. One is the carrier whose identity has been established, and the other participant represents meaning or identity. Followed by Pierce's typology of signs on the basis of the degree of conventionality of signs, symbols refer to a mode in which the signifier does not resemble the signified but which is fundamentally arbitrary or purely conventional. Therefore, the symbolic suggestive process involving "one participant, the carrier" (Kress & Van Leeuwen, 1996), and its symbolic meaning should be displayed by necessary verbal elaborations. In Figure 39, for example, Obama declares that **instead of losing jobs, we have created them over more than** 4.2 **million so far** in this video. With the help of the demonstration in the diagram in Image 3, direct and convincing illustration about the increasing number of new jobs in the past two years can be noticed by the audience.

The following example is selected from Romney's attack against Obama's loose policy towards trade with China. The symbolic meaning of national flags is conventionally assumed to be the sign of a nation. Without explanation in verbal modes, it is impossible for the viewers to understand the real meaning of the symbols in such a new context. Visually, the national flags of US and China printed on cubes can initially draw the viewers' attention and interest. Later, Wane and wax of their size impresses Americans a lot. Verbally, the relational processes are employed to attribute its symbolic meaning at the beginning, which gives the viewers clear and precise definition. Exact numbers printed in the image enhance its persuasive and objective force. Apparently, the communicative effect can be strengthened by the collaboration between verbal and visual modes as the viewers' subjective experience and objective understanding can be realized simultaneously.

Failing American Workers 1   Failing American Workers 2   Failing American Workers 3
Failing American Workers 4   Failing American Workers 5   Failing American Workers 6
Failing American Workers 7   Failing American Workers 8   Failing American Workers 9

Figure 40　Failing American Workers

7.5　Extension on Interpersonal Meaning

Another typical aspect in specification in both positive and negative televised political advertising appears in the extension of the speakers' identity, social relations and their attitudes which can be realized through the collaboration between interpersonal meaning in verbal modes and interactive meaning in visual modes.

7.5.1　Extension on Identity

Identity extension involves in the complement of the interpersonal functions in the text through the collaboration with interactive meaning in the visual modes. Statistics indicate that the consistency in the distribution in both mood system and modality systems can mirror the similar communicative intentions. For the main purpose of televised political advertising is to inform, different responsibilities are distributed to representative

Chapter Ⅶ Meaning-making in Verbal-Visual Interaction

participants and their viewers. Therefore, both "declarative clauses" in verbal modes and "offer images" in visual modes account for the largest proportion respectively, to make the advertising more objective, informative and persuasive. For this sake, viewers are assumed to be spectators. For interrogative and imperative clauses aiming to get the corresponding feedbacks from the audience, "demand images" with direct eye contact are preferred. In the fourth image, in Figure 41, Hillary Clinton looking at the camera and saying **People asked me, what will be different if I am president,** the design aims to elaborates a question and answer procedure as if she would have answered the question raised by the viewers in a direct way. Senses of involvement and intimacy can be reinforced.

Designs of the typical image on the screen along with the ritual self-introduction and approval of the message declared by the advertiser can be regarded as the specification of the different positive identities memorable to the viewers. Along with Hillary Clinton's self-introduction at the end of her positive advertising (Image 9) entitled **Families First,** it can be noted that Clinton wraps a little girl in her arm, looking at her lovingly. Hillary Clinton being a mother and presidential candidate, her image of a female president who puts families first is stressed, approved and instantiated, which can deepen the viewers' impression and win over their appreciation.

To be the American President, all the candidates are expected to have the similar characteristics: decisive in action, sober but optimistic in crisis, kind to his people, harsh to dangers and energetic in movement while preaching their future policies and eulogizing their personalities. Thus, visual modes are important channels to achieve the communicative effect, giving the voters visualized and real experiences. In addition, stereotypes of their images are fixed through the repetitive appearance of good images in positive advertising and bad images in negative advertising which must be more memorable than their names mentioned in linguistic form only.

Figure 41　Families First

7.5.2　Extension on Social Relations

Different social relations can also be simultaneously constructed and extended through the choice of personal pronouns in verbal modes and the size of frames in visual modes. In terms of establishing social relations through interpersonal function, the agreement can be arrived at between visual and verbal modes. Selections of personal pronouns in texts often go along with corresponding tactics in images. Direct eye contact with the viewers taken from a close-up shot or a frontal angle have the same communication effect as such inclusive pronouns **we**, **our**, **us** do in communication, indicating involvement, solidarity and alignment. For example, in Clinton's positive advertising entitled **Tomorrow**, Hillary Clinton, facing to the camera, talked about her duty and plan as the future American president, encouraged the voters to work together with her and asked for their votes. Several kinds of social relations have been assumed to Clinton. She is a candidate, a future American president and an American citizen. Statistics indicate that she mainly used first-person pronouns and

Chapter Ⅶ   Meaning-making in Verbal-Visual Interaction

second-person pronouns as no third party had been involved in her speech. Visually, close-up shots and frontal angles are selected. Fictive social and power relations can be perceived by viewers. Balance of her power and solidarity in her advertising has been kept well by verbal-visual interactions.

On the contrary, images taken from a long shot or a side-on angle usually have similar implications implied in the third-person pronouns, suggesting divergence, detachment and individualism. Take Trump's negative advertising, *Unfit*, for example. Corresponding to the third-person pronouns referring to Hillary Clinton, no eye contact and frontal angel take place in the video. Therefore, the viewers' senses of alienation towards Clinton have been reinforced through verbal-visual interactions.

Degrees of verbal inclusion and visual involvement combined in this way can be interpreted as video advertisers are inclined to create a high level of involvement or detachment with viewers through interactions between verbal mode and visual mode.

7.5.3   Extension on Attitude

According to Thompson, "Attitude is used by the language users to show their emotional response to people and events, and appraise them from the emotional perspective." (2008). Modal auxiliaries in verbal modes and modality markers in visual modes are reliable indicators suggesting such attitudes toward the values of reality, possibility and necessity. For example, consistent with the self-praise to their policies and personalities in positive advertising, naturalistic colors and contextualization are adopted. On the contrary, non-naturalistic colors and de-contextualization accompany with their attack against their rivals in negative advertising.

Linguistic forms are restricted in their possibilities and precision to trigger or express emotions, visual modes can be a necessary complement by means of non-verbal communication, color saturations and contextualization. From the perspective of multimodal discourse analysis, communications can take place not only in written or oral forms but in otherforms of signs that can be expressed, perceived and interpreted by human beings with five sensory channels, including visual sensory, auditive sensory, tactile sensory, olfactory sensory and gustatory sensory.

It is congruent to Mehrabian's (1968) study that 93% of daily communications depends on non-verbal communication, among of which facial expressions and gestures are the most effective way to express emotions; 7% of them rely on linguistic form. Compared with tradition printed media, the application of television makes it possible to realize both verbal and non-verbal interactions in televised political adverting. Therefore, the represented participants' facial expressions and gestures are indispensable complements to synthesis of meaning-making. Though non-verbal communication is culture-based, the universalities still exist. It can be noted that eyes and faces functions as the most attractive parts in expressing feelings.

Ekman (2003) identifying seven universal facial expressions: anger, disgust, sadness, fear, surprise, contempt and happiness, those facial expressions in the image matching with different gazes can generate various interactive meaning. For example, it has been confirmed that the plural forms of first person pronouns and close-up shots can enhance the intimacy, solidarity and alignment. However, statistics in Table 27 show that more close-up shots have been used in negative advertising than positive ones mainly because the viewers are more likely to be infected by negative facial expressions in a short distance as if their privacy and personal interests were to be invaded; senses of horror, sadness, disgust, distrust, etc. will be initiated. On the contrary, positive facial expressions in positive advertising can mirror the represented participants' inner minds, facilitating the consolidation of intimate relations with the viewers.

Being the essential and fundamental elements in the perception of the real physical world, colors are considered as "the substance of how we experience the environment" (Meerwein, 2007). The influence of various colors upon the psyche of human beings has been confirmed. Kouwer (1949) manages an experimental and phenomenological study of the "character" of the colors, in which it has been proved that color has the "potentials and possibilities" to "make an appeal to the others and thus constitute the very

Chapter VII Meaning-making in Verbal-Visual Interaction

situation". According to Elliot (2015), certain colors can produce systematic physiological reactions manifesting "emotional experience (e. g. negative arousal), cognitive orientation (e. g. outward focus), and overt action e. g. forceful behavior)". Variables in color saturation in televised political advertising can be a significant complement to the theme in the texts. The intensified emotions and atmosphere implied in bright and full colors can impose direct stimulations upon the viewers' visual sensory. However, negative attitudes, such as, sadness, depression, terror, etc. often go along with weakened degrees of color saturation, which can influence the viewers' mental state. Consequently, equivalent reactions can be aroused and their memories of linguistic descriptions can be consolidated.

The degrees of contextualization determine how much information in the text is visualized in the image. It is another factor in expressing the producers' attitude as well as compensating for less significant background information excluded in the text. In addition, the viewers are urged to follow the image-producers' focus on information distributed in the text as well as the image. Therefore, for the same texts with corresponding images, the degrees of contextualization can have different effects on the viewers' emotions and cognition towards the televised political advertising. Collaborated with verbal modes, the absence of contexts in the pictures can effectively make lexical or visual features prominent in the images.

It is a common sense that people have more confidence in what they have seen than what they have heard in the daily life as it is declared that seeing is believing. Schlesinger (1992) insists that dynamic pictures can reflect actuality and "a medium through which reality can be genuinely and authentically captured and presented" in a manner that is optimally suited to the medium. For the effectiveness in spreading information, correlated experimental studies (Gunter 1987, Graber 1990) reveal that longer memories of information happen to the viewers through television. More attention has been paid to dynamic images than words as long as the viewers turn on their television. Therefore, the influence of televised political advertising upon the viewers' behavior and cognition can be affirmed.

7.6　Ideology and Power in Visual-verbal Interactions

Van Dijk (1995) treats discourse analysis as ideology analysis in essence as he holds that ideology is typically, though not exclusively, expressed and reproduced in discourse and communication, including visual semiotic messages, such as pictures, photographs and movies. Ideological analysis in MCDA consists of three parts, namely, social analysis, cognitive analysis and discourse analysis: The social analysis pertains to the context, discourse analysis needs to be text based and cognitive analysis should include social cognition and personal cognition.

In MCDA, ideology and power are taken as important aspects of establishing and maintaining control and dominance in communication. Ideologies form the basic social representations of the beliefs shared by a group, and precisely function as the framework that defines the overall coherence of these beliefs (Van Dijk, 2004). Political discourse analysis should be based on the exploration into the underlying ideologies. In addition, it should combine the analysis on structures of discourse with social cognition, for the purpose of probing into how ideological discourse serves to sustain social identity, social order and social recognition. Thus, the deep-rooted ideologies allow new social opinions to be easily inferred, acquired and distributed in a group when the group and its members are confronted with new events and situations. More importantly, it also forms a certain kind of mindset, cognitively or prototype, in which the manipulation of social power is functions.

Previous analysis in this study suggests that studies on the exploration upon unfolded ideology and power relations in visual-verbal interactions in both positive and negative televised campaign advertising should be context-based and function-orientated. In other words, elements in the multimodal discourses such as background, identities, intentions, values or beliefs

Chapter Ⅶ Meaning-making in Verbal-Visual Interaction

should be taken into consideration.

Following basic values and beliefs of American people since the issue of Declaration of Independence with its focus on "freedom, democracy and Liberty", all the advertisers adopt similar strategies to achieve ideological control over their potential voters, their multimodal designs with distinctive features aiming to influence the voters' judgment and selection. The way how those different semiotic resources are chosen and assembled in meaning making can determine the communication of ideas, values and identities, and constrain different kinds of interactions. The crucial implication here is that meanings and semiotic systems are shaped by social structures, and that as social structures shift in society, our languages and other systems of socially accepted meanings can and do change.

When the social relations in America are mentioned, Thomas Jefferson claimed in the Declaration of Independence that "men are created equal, that they are endowed by the creator with certain unalienable rights that among these are life, liberty and the pursuit of happiness". Therefore, intimate and equal social relations need to be constructed between the politicians and the public in the US.

The main purpose of televised campaign advertising is to persuade the viewers to accept their leadership through the concrete elaboration of their actions and behaviors from the perspective of verbal and visual modes. Great significance should be given to the construction of their identities. Identities refer to their social position they have taken for granted. Critical linguistics, with its purpose of unfolding the relations between discourse and identities, reveals that certain norms can be obeyed or rebelled for the building of social actors ideologically. In political discourses, politicians tend to assume different representations based on their communication intentions. In different contexts, their identities and relations with the audience can be arbitrarily highlighted, exaggerated, and fixed to influence the judgment of the public and thus achieve their aims of ideological control.

Politicians try to emphasize their equal identities and distinctive merits which are also possessed by average American citizens, to shorten the social distance and win over their admiration and support by positive self-presentations. In addition, the more objective, neutral and naturalistic points of view are adopted in positive advertising because they try to enhance the persuasive forces of their words and performances through the seemingly authentic and objective designs. Therefore, verbal and visual expressions of their excessively intensified emotions are avoided as a balance can be kept between persuasive forces of emotional appreciation and rational judgment endowed to their viewers. Adaptive to American, culture which emphasizes freedom, equality and democracy, strategies, indicating overwhelming dominance and control upon the public, are avoided in their designs of visual-verbal interactions. In terms of the ideational function, they both mainly employed material andrelational processes and their wording was ideology-based. In terms of the interpersonal function, the declarative clauses were most frequently used for the purpose of increasing the objectivity and credibility of their speeches; the modal auxiliary verbs, emphasizing their ability, power, resolution and obligation; the personal pronoun "we" constructing intimate relationship with their audience. Analogically, visual modes in positive advertising contribute to specifying, extending or consolidating the meaning implied in words. Offer images are more frequently used than demand images for the enhancement of its objectivity. Distance kept between the represented participants and the viewers is neither too short nor too far for the sake of balancing solidarity and power via proper selections of size of frame and perspectives. Modality markers with high modality present the viewers with a much more naturalistic angle towards the images, its objectivity and authenticity, thus, can encourage the viewers to make a correct judgment. In a word, repetitive appearance of the same meaning-potential blended in the interaction of verbal and visual modes helps to reinforce its persuasive force to achieve ideological control over the viewers finally.

On the other hand, positive self-presentation is usually combined with negative other-presentation or known as derogation, following the well-known social psychology of ingroup-outgroup polarization. Their rivals in

Chapter VII Meaning-making in Verbal-Visual Interaction

negative televised campaign advertising are assumed completely different identities in terms of interpersonal and interactive meanings. Similar to positive advertising, the construction of their rivals' identity in negative advertising depends on the elaboration on facts, truth or actions related to them. Therefore, material processes and declarative clauses in texts and the "offer image" in the images account for the largest proportion. The most distinctive feature in negative advertising lies in its emphasis on its extension on attitudes in terms of visual modes. Intensified negative attitudes and sympathetic feelings towards the main characters in negative advertising are highlighted and exaggerated as the main participants are candidates of the other parties and their victims or opponents through the description of their actions and behavior. Non-naturalistic designs in images can make their speeches sound emphatic, peremptory, opinionated and unfriendly. The emphatic features highlighted in the visual images can give viewers' permanent memories.

  Power in discourse isrelevant to discourse as a place where relations of power are actually exercised and enacted. Participants involved in political advertising are not equal in social ranks; the inequality is called an unequal encounter. Naturally, not all the people have got the same opportunity to approach to the media or to medical, legal, political, bureaucratic or scholarly text and talk. Therefore, the measures of discourse access may be rather faithful indicators of the power of social groups and their members. More powerful participants possibly treat social practice in a dominant way, controlling the construction and deconstruction of both verbal and visual communication. In the process of the American presidential election, both of the candidates, therefore, are endowed with two kinds of power, power-to as well as power-over. As for those candidates themselves, on one hand, they can have access to the power with which they can exercise and enact their influence upon the public in discourse, which is known as "discourse power"; on the other hand, they aim to manipulate thoughts of the public partly due to their prestigious social status and partly due to their political rhetoric. Moreover, televised presidential campaign advertising also represents a kind of social struggle in discourse. As power, "in" discourse or "behind" discourse, is not permanent and undisputed attribute of any one person or social grouping (Fairclough, 2001), those who hold the power have to evaluate their power continuously, whereas those without power, in turn, constantly ask for power. Such a phenomenon can be mirrored by the style of the discourse. Data show that the candidates, consciously or unconsciously, adjusted their strategies of argumentation to the changing situations in order to win the power. However, it has to be noted that the control over orders of discourse in power struggle, is a powerful mechanism for sustaining power, and the struggle of the working class is still slave to these orders.

Therefore, the publication of televised political advertising suggests their prominent social positions in power. Great importance should be given to the authenticity and reality which can be other indicators of power relation as Nesler (1993) claims that the public are inclined to accept the information coming from the authoritative recourses, such as officials, experts, scholars and etc. One of the greatest distinctive features in televised political advertising is that the advertisers as well as their aliens themselves are engaged in the film of the advertising. Therefore, the multimodal selections in positive advertising are more objective and reliable than those in negative advertising so as to consolidate their power relations with the viewers. Comparatively, the performances of their rivals in the negative advertising are more irrational, emotional and subjective, stressing that their rivals fail to manipulate the power. Senses of vagueness and unsteadiness have been delivered to the viewers, which harm American democracy.

Hodge and Kress (1988) stress the growing importance of sound and visual images and declare that multimodal interaction cannot assume "that texts produce exactly the meanings and effects that their authors hope for: it is precisely the struggles and their uncertain outcomes that must be studies at the level of social action, and their effects in the production of meaning". Human communication, the purpose of realizing certain kinds of communicative purposes through verbal or non-verbal communication, doesn't depend on

Chapter VII Meaning-making in Verbal-Visual Interaction

the literal meaning (denotative meaning) or is limited to the discourses, the authors or the readers themselves. Instead, it relies on the interaction, interpretation and negotiation made by both speakers and hearers in a dynamic process of contextual construction which can reflect the relationship between the ideological control of the dominant group and resistance of the dominated group in society.

Chapter VIII
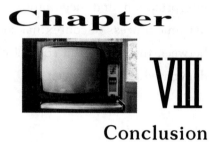
Conclusion

8.1 Contribution of the Study

Since most of the previous studies only conducted a mono-modal analysis upon televised political advertising without a critical point of view, the present study contributes to the advancement in three aspects, namely, the formulation of an analytical model upon multimodal political advertising, the improvement of public communion and the enhancement of linguistic awareness.

Firstly, through the comparative studies upon positive and negative televised political advertising in terms of both verbal and visual modes, the present study verifies the applicability and relevance of Halliday's SFG and Kress and Van Leeuwen's VG in studying meaning potentials in televised political advertising. Figure 37 provides a framework for the analysis of televised advertising with political intentions. In this framework, the first step is to gather the verbal and visual data from the advertising. Any televised political advertising is to be divided into two parts: texts transcript from the video and image grasped from the dynamic films. Then, concrete analysis upon the variables in both texts and images should be done under the instruction of VG and SFG. Next, elements in verbal and visual modes should be combined for the further study upon interaction between two modes. Corresponding to participants and verbs in ideational function, three elements in the image should be identified, that is, who speaks (reference), what happens (events) and what exists. As for interpersonal extension, meaning beyond the words should be identified. Relevant to interpersonal meaning implied in the meaning-potential, several factors should be studied, namely, its degree of relevance with shaping of identity, the assumed social relations between the elements and their viewers as well as the attitudinal meaning, like facial expressions, body movement, modality markers. Finally, the comprehensive analysis can reveal the meanings and stances buried in the texts and images. Thus, the advertisers' power and ideology can be exposed via relating to circumstances, identities of participants as well as common cultures, beliefs and values shared with the public.

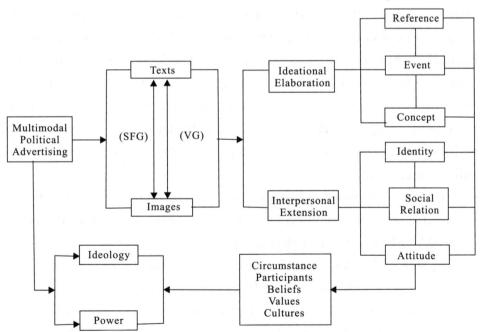

Figure 42   Model for Analyzing Televised Political Advertising

Secondly, the characteristics exposed in the both positive and negative advertising are also helpful and instructive in the process of public communion so as to achieve certain communicative intentions. Different political intentions taken into consideration, it exposed various buried meanings not only in linguistic forms but also in other elements, such as construction of images, color, brightness andetc in visual modes. Studies on the interaction between two modes led to more precise and accurate understanding and interpretation upon political televised advertising. On one hand, the advertisers can know how to choose and combine different verbal and visual elements to win over the favor of the viewers. On the other hand, they can avoid misunderstanding, offence and discomfort in their advertisements.

Thirdly, the greatest contribution lies in its "critical studies" upon televised political adverting. It revealed the strategies of meaning-making through a certain system of verbal or visual signs in specific social and cultural circumstances, and treated the televised political advertising as a social practice for effective ideological control and power manipulation. The exposure of cognitive factors in televised political adverting can enhance the linguistic awareness of the public, namely, their consciousness and sensitivity to the forms and functions of language used in our daily and social life. Visual modes treated as a corresponding approach of communication, the present study can encourage the public to improve their awareness of multimodal signs so as to avoid bewilderment in the flood of false multimodal political propaganda.

Therefore, several conclusions about the composition of different modes in televised political advertising can finally be arrived at from the perspective of MCDA, which have been elaborated in detail.

To start with, multimodal resources applied in the production of any televised political advertising should consist of both the verbal and non-verbal modes. The former refers to the linguistic system of communication in both oral and textual forms such as monologue, dialogues, interviews, slogans, off-screen voices, screen texts and so on. The latter one, as non-linguistic system of communication, is composed of the visual modes including color saturation, framing, shape, body movement, and the focus of the lens and the vocal modes including background music, timbre, and

Chapter Ⅷ   Conclusion

sound effect and the like. The combination of these two multimodal resources, functioning as multimodal choices in meaning-making, should be taken into consideration in multimodal discourse analysis.

Moreover, it can be safely assumed that the more modes the advertising employs, the more informative it will be, as any change of the symbolic expressions can generate new meaning. However, it doesn't mean that any addition or subtraction of different modes in televised political advertising can be treated as a simple calculation of meaning-making that can strengthen the communicative force. In other words, those multimodal resources are not organized randomly but artistically and artificially. Modes with their respective characteristics, known as multimodal complexity, should be arranged in an appropriate way (Boeriis, 2008). Generally speaking, the verbal modes are still the dominant parts in political discourse for its primary requirement of the authenticity, objectivity and exactness of the information. The non-verbal modes are necessary counterparts which play decisive roles in the substitution, illustration, extension, salience, empathy and rhetoric of the information transmitted by linguistic forms. All in all, the tactic multimodal choices and collaborations in political adverting aim to maximize its communicative potential by the realization of "meaning potential" in the process of meaning-making in certain contexts.

Thirdly, being consistent with the ideas and values of the dominant group, the multimodal designs in televised political advertising, as another kind of social practice, should fundamentally contribute to the realization of their social, cultural and political interests. In terms of the distribution of power in society, its imparity determines the situation that not everyone has the equal opportunity to have access to social resources. Let us take the mass media for example. For better manipulation of the thought, those multimodal resources in mass media, for instance, television, newspapers, magazines and etc. , can be deliberately and arbitrarily abused to generate meanings that are naturalized in form, but ideological in content. The study of the stylistics on televised political advertising should not only be confined to the linguistic study itself but also be extended to the demonstration of the meaning-making process of all signs, taking the historical, cultural, social and political elements into consideration.

Though it can be said with certainty that the delivery of meaning through multimodality is a more efficient and explicit way, its influence upon the receiver's actions is not absolute, as not every voter can be influenced by the televised political advertising. Just as Machin and Mayr (2012) proposed that communication in language is based, as in the Sapir-whorf model, on the idea that "everyone agrees to use the same words to mean the same thing", no natural relationship exists between what you say and what you mean, but "a concept can be established by the people through long social practice". A conclusion can be arrived here that the influence in verbal mode in Sapir-whorf Hypothesis can be extended to a large scale in non-verbal mode, because in the process of meaning production and perception they have the same mechanism in which the producers, abiding by a certain cultural and contextual conventions or rules, can make and understand reasonable semiotic choices in social interactions, which can be understood by the receivers.

Therefore, the study of those multimodal modes in political advertising must be encoded and decoded in an ideological way, culture and thought taken into consideration. It possibly displays a certain kind of power relation. Apart from the explicit meaning on the surface, therefore, the strong "political intentions" buried in them should be studied and identified in a critical way.

8.2 Recommendations

Besides the major findings presented above, some noticeable limitations and suggestions in the present studies should be pointed out:

Firstly, for the corpus-based study of televised political adverting, only 21 pieces for either positive or negative advertising were analyzed in the present research. The limited number of selected data is far from exhaustive to cover every aspect and expose characteristics in details. More campaign advertising should be collected and analyzed and a precise quantitative analysis should be expected as it is emphasized that one of the criticisms of CDA lies in its focus on "qualitative methods of inquiry instead of employment of quantitative and comparative methods" (Machin and Mayr, 2012).

Secondly, though quantitative research method was employed, Software, like Antconc, is restricted to small part of the research, such as modal auxiliaries, personal pronouns and etc. Hopefully, more quantitative research methods will be introduced to the study of all the variables in both visual and verbal modes.

Thirdly, while CDA or MCDA focuses on ideologically driven discrimination, with respect to gender, ethnicity, class and related social variables, it should be noted that a new positive and optimistic trend that artificial meaning-making functions to "make the world a better place" defined as "Positive Discourse Analysis (PDA)" (cf. Martin and Rose, 2003) should be taken into consideration in future studies in multimodal discourse analysis of public discourses. It can be safely assumed that successful design of televised political advertising can facilitate the construction of better interpersonal relationship as well as lead to innovations of a better world, which are consistent with two fundamental themes in PDA, namely, solidarity and change.

References

Althusser, L. (1971) Ideology and Ideological State Apparatuses: Notes Towards an Investigation, in L. Althusser (ed.), *Lenin and Other Essays*. London: New Left Books.

Bakhtin, M. M. (1981a.) *The Dialogic Imagination*. Austin, TX: University of Texas Press.

Barthes, R. *Elements of Semiology*. (1964/1973) Tran. By Annette lavers and Colin Smith, New York: Hill and Wang.

Barthes, R. (1977)*Rhetoric of the Image*. London: Collins.

Barthes, R. (1977)*Image-Music-Text*. London: Fontana.

Basil, M. , Schooler, C. , & Reeves, B. (1991) Positive and Negative Political Advertising: Effectiveness of advertising and perceptions of candidates. In F. Biocca (Ed.), *Television and Political Advertising* (vol. 1, 245—262).

Baker, P. , & McEnery, T. (2005) A Corpus-based Approach to Discourses of Refugees and Asylum Seekers in UN and Newspaper Texts. *Journal of Language and Politics* 4(2), 197—226.

Benoit, W. L. (1999) Seeing Spots:*A Functional Analysis of Presidential Television Advertisements in* 1952—1996. New York: Praeger.

Benoit, W. L. , Mchale, J. P. , Hansen, J. L. & Pier, P. M. (2003) *Campaign* 2000: *A Functional Analysis of Presidential Campaign Discourse Advertisements*. New York: Praeger.

References

Bezemer, J., Mavers, D. (2011) Multimodal Transcription as Academic Practice: A Social Semiotic Perspective. *International Journal of Social Research Methodology*, 14(3): 191—207.

Boeriisb, Morten (2008) Mastering Multimodal Complexity Systemic Functional Linguistics in Use. *Odense Working Papers in Language and Communication* vol. 29, 219.

Brown, R. and A. Gilman (1960) The Pronouns of Power and Solidarity. In T. Sebeok (ed.), *Style in Language*. Cambridge, MA: MIT Press, 253—276.

Cook, G. (2002). *The Discourse of Advertising 2nd edn*. London: Routledge.

Cronkhite, G., Liska, J., & Schrader, D. (1991) Toward an integration of textual and response analysis applied to the 1988 presidential campaign. In F. Biocca (Ed.), *Television and Political Advertising* (vol. 2, pp. 163—84). Hills-dale, NJ: Erlbaum.

Cundy, D. T. (1986) Political Commercials and Candidate Image: The Effect Can Be Substantial. In L. L. Kaid, D. Nimmo, & K. R. Sanders (Eds.), *New Perspectives on Political Advertising* (pp. 210 — 234). Carbondale: Southern Illinois Press.

Descutner, D., Burnier, D., Mickunas, A., & Letteri, R. (1991) Bad Signs and Cryptic Codes in a Postmodern World: A Semiotic Analysis of the Dukakis Advertising. In F. Biocca (Ed.), *Television and Political Advertising* (vol. 2, pp. 93—114). Hillsdale, NJ: Erlbaum.

Devlin, L. P. (2001) Contrasts in Presidential Campaign Commercials of 2000, *US Behavioral Scientist*, 44, 2338—2369.

Dewey, Caitlin. (2016) "Facebook Fake-News Writer: I Think Donald Trump Is in the White House because of Me". *Washington Post*, November, 17.

Ekman, P. (2003) Emotion Revealed: *Recognizing Faces and Feelings to Improve Communication and Emotional Life*. New York: Times Books.

Fairclough, N. (1989) *Language and Power*. London: Longman.

Fairclough, N. (1995) *Critical Discourse Analysis: The Critical study of Language*. London: Longman.

Firth, J. R. (1930) *Speech*. Oxford University Press.

Foote, J. S. (1991) Implications of Presidential Communication for Electoral Success. In L. L. Kaid, J. Gerstle, & K. R. Sanders (Eds.), *Mediated Politics in Two Cultures: Presidential Campaigning in the United States and France*, 261—270. New York: Praeger.

Forceville, C & Urios-Aparisi, E. (2018) *Multimodal Methaphor*. Shanghai: Shanghai Foreign Language Education Press

Garramone, G. M., & Smith, S. J. (1984) Reactions to Political Advertising: Clarifying Sponsor Effects. *Journalism Quarterly*, 51, 771—775.

Garramone, G. M. (1985) Effects of Negative Political Advertising: The Roles of Sponsor and Rebuttal. *Journal of Broadcasting and Electronic Media*, 29, 147—159.

Garramone, G. M., Atkin, C. K., Pinkleton, B. E., & Cole, R. T. (1990) Effects of Negative Political Advertising on the Political Process. *Journal of Broadcasting and Electronic Media*, 34, 299—311.

Geis, M. L. (1982). *The Language of Television Advertising*. New York: Academic Press.

Ghorpade, S. (1986). Agenda Setting: A Test of Advertising's Neglected Function. *Journal of Advertising Research*, 26, 23—27.

Graber, A. (1990). Seeing Is Remembering: How Visuals Contribute to Learning from Television News. *Journal of Communication*. 40, 134—155.

Griffin, M., & Kagan, S. (1996). Picturing Culture in Political Spots: 1992 Campaigns in Israel and the United States. *Political Communication*, 13, 43—61.

Gunter, Barrie. (1987). *Poor Reception: Misunderstanding and Forgetting Broadcast News*. Hillsdale: Lawrence Erlbaum Associates.

Halliday, M. A. K. (1985). *An Introduction to Functional Grammar*. London: Edward Arnold.

Halliday, M. A. K. (1994) *An Introduction to Functional Grammar (Second Edition)*. London: Edward Arnold.

Halliday, M. A. K. (1973) *Explorations in the Functions of Language*. London: Edward Arnold.

Halliday, M. A. K. (2001) *Language as Social Semiotic: The Social Interpersonal Interpretation of Language and Meaning*. Beijing: Foreign Language Teaching and Research Press.

Halliday, M. A. K. (2003) On the "Architecture" of Human Language. *On Language and Linguistics*. Volume 3 in the Collected Works of M. A. K. Halliday. London and New York: Equinox.

Halliday, M. A. K. , & Matthiessen, C. M. I. M. (2004) *An Introduction to Functional Grammar (third edition)*. London: Hodder Arnold.

Hart Christopher. (2005) Analyzing Political Discourse: Toward a Cognitive Approach. *Critical Discourse Studies* 2 (2): 189—194

Hodge, Robert & Gunther Kress. (1988) *Social Semiotics*. Cambridge: Polity.

Holtz-Bacha, C. ,Kaid, L. L. , & Johnston, A. (1994) Political Television Advertising in Western Democracies: A Comparison of Campaign Broadcasts in the Unites States, Germany and France. *Political Communication*, 11, 67—80.

Holtz-Bacha, C. , &Kaid, L. L. (1995) A Comparative Perspective on Political Advertising. In L. L. Kaid & C. Holtz-Bacha (Eds.), *Political Advertising in Western Democracies: Parties and Candidates on Television* (8—18). Thousand Oaks, CA: Sage.

Hodge, B. and Kress, G. (1993) *Language as Ideology*. London: Routledge.

Iedema, R. (2003) Multimodality, Resemiotization: Extending the Analysis of Discourse as Multi-Semiotic Practice. *Visual Communication*, 2, 29—57.

Iedema, R. (2003) *Multimodality, Resemiotization: Extending the Analysis of Discourse as Multi-semiotic Practice*. London: Sage.

Jewitt, C. (2009) An Introduction to Multimodality. In: Jewitt, C. (ed.) *The Routledge Handbook of Multimodal Analysis*. London: Routledge, 14—27.

Johnston, A. (1991) Political Broadcasts: An analysis of Form, Content, and Style in Presidential Communication. In L. L. Kaid, J. Gerstle, & K. R. Sanders (Eds.), *Mediated politics in two cultures: Presidential Campaigning in the United States and France* (59—72). New York: Praeger.

Kress, G., & Van Leeuwen, T. (1996) *Reading Images: The Grammar of Visual Design*. London: Routledge.

Kress, G., & Van Leeuwen, T. (2001) *Multimodal Discourse: The Modes and Media of Contemporary Communication*. London: Bloomsbury.

Kress, G., & Van Leeuwen, T. (2006) *Reading Images: The Grammar of Visual Design* (2rd). London: Routledge.

Kaid, L. L., & Sanders, K. R. (1978) Political Television Commercials: An Experimental Study of Type and Length. *Communication Research*, 5, 57—70.

Kaid, L. L., Nimmo, D., & Sanders, K. R. (Eds.) (1986) *New Perspectives on Political Advertising*. Carbondale: Southern Illinois Press.

Kaid, L. L. (1991) The Effects of Television Broadcasts on Perceptions of Presi-dential Candidates in the United States and France. In L. L. Kaid, J. Gerstle, & K. R. Sanders (Eds.), *Mediated Politics in Two Cultures: Presidential Campaigning in the United States and France* (247—260). New York: Praeger.

Kaid, L. L., Leland, C. M., & Whitney, S. (1992) The Impact of Televised Political Advertising: Evoking Viewer Responses in the 1988 Presidential Campaign. *Southern Communication Journal*, 57, 285—295.

Kaid, L. L., & Holtz-Bacha, C. (1995a) An Introduction to Parties and Candidates on Television. In L. L. Kaid & C. Holtz-Bacha (Eds.), *Political Advertising in Western Democracies: Parties and Candidates on Television* (1—7). Thousand Oaks, CA: Sage.

Kaid, L. L. (1997) Effects of the Television Spots on Images of Dole and Clinton. *US Behavioral Scientist*, 40, 1085—1094.

Kaid, L. L., & Dimitrova, D. V. (2005) The Television Advertising

Battleground in the 2004 Presidential Election, *Journalism Studies*, 6 (3), 165—175

Kaid, L. L. & Holtz-Bacha, H. (2006) *The Sage Handbook of Political Advertising*. London: Sage.

Kern, M. (1989) 30 *Second Politics: Political Advertising in the Eighties*. New York: Praeger.

Kress, G. (1976) "Introduction", in G. Kress (ed.) *Halliday: System and Function in Language*, vii-xxi. Oxford: Oxford University Press. London: Sage.

Lakoff, R. (1990) *Talking Power: The Politics of Language in Our Lives*. USA: Basic Books

Lang, A. (1991) Emotion, Formal Features, and Memory for Televised Political Advertisements. In F. Biocca (Ed.), *Television and Political Advertising*, vol. 1, 221—243. Hillsdale, NJ: Erlbaum.

Loden, A. D. (1989) Political Advertising Bibliography. *Political Communication Review*, 14, 19—46.

Machin, D. & Van Leeuwen, T. (2007) *Global Media Discourse: A Critical Introduction*. Abingdon: Routledge.

Machin, D., & Mayr, A. (2012) *How to Do Critical Discourse Analysis: A Multimodal Introduction*. London: Sage.

Machin, David (2013) Introduction: What is Multimodal Critical Discourse Studies? *Critical Discourse Studies*, 4, 10.

Martin, J., R., and Rose, D. (2003) *Working with Discourse: Meaning Beyond the Clause*. London, New York: Continuum.

Meadow, R. G., & Sigelman, L. (1982) Some Effects and Non-effects of Campaign Commercials: An Experimental Study. *Political Behavior*, 4, 163—175.

Merelman, R. M. (1986) Revitalizing Political Socialization. In M. G. Hermann (ed.), *Political Psychology*. San Francisco, Jossey-Bass. 279—319. Experimental Study. *Political Behavior*, 4, 163—75.

Newhagen, J. E., & Reeves, B. (1991) Emotion and Memory Responses for Negative Political Advertising: A Study of Television Commercials

Used in the 1988 Presidential Election. In F. Biocca (Ed.), *Television and Political Advertising* (vol. 1, 197—220). Hillsdale, NJ: Erlbaum.

O'Halloran, K. L. (2011) Multimodal Analysis Within an Interactive Software Environment: Critical Discourse Perspective. *Critical Discourse Studies* 8(2): 109—125.

Parkinson, Hannah Jane. 2016 "Click and Elect: How Fake News Helped Donald Trump Win a Real Election" Guardian, November 14.

Patterson, T. E., & McClure, R. D. (1976) *The Unseeing Eye: The Myth of Television Power in National Politics*. New York: Putnam.

Paul, C. & Christina, S. (2011) Discourse and Politics. *Discourse Studies* Vol. 3, 303—329.

Reisigl, M. & Wodak, R. (2001) *Discourse and Discrimination*. London: Routledge.

Roberts, M., & McCombs, M. (1994) Agenda Setting and Political Advertising: Origins of the News Agenda. *Political Communication*, 11, 249—262.

Simpsom, P. (1993) *Language, Ideology and Point of View*. London; New York: Routledge.

Schleuder, J., McCombs, M., & Wanta, W. (1991) Inside the Agenda-setting Process: How Political Advertising and TV News Prime Viewers to Think about Issues and Candidates. In F. Biocca (Ed.), *Television and Political Advertising* (vol. 1, 265—309). Hillsdale, NJ: Erlbaum.

Thorson, E., Christ, W. G., & Caywood, C. (1991) Effects of Issue-image Strategies, Attack and Support Appeals, Music, and Visual Content in Political Commercials. *Journal of Broadcasting and Electronic Media*, 35, 465—486.

Van Dijk, T. A. (1993) Principles of Critical Discourse Analysis. *Discourse and Society*. 4(2), 249—283.

Van Dijk, T. A. (1995) Ideological Discourse Analysis. http://www.discourses.org/download/articles/143.

Van Dijk, T. A. (1995) Discourse Analysis as Ideology Analysis. http://

www. daneprairie. com. 17.

Van Dijk, T. A. (1996) Discourse, Power and Access. In Carmen Rosa Caldas-Coulthard and Malcolm Coulthard (Eds.), *Texts and Practices. Readings in Critical Discourse Analysis*. 84—104. London: Routledge,.

Van Dijk, T. A. (1997a) Cognitive Context Models and Discourse. *Language Structure, Discourse and the Access to Consciousness*. Amsterdam, Benjamins. 189—226.

Van Dijk, T. A. (1997b) What Is Political Discourse Analysis? *Political Linguistics*. Amsterdam, Benjamins. pp. 11—52.

Van Dijk, T. A. (1997) *Discourse as Structure and Process: Discourse Studies: A Multidisciplinary Introduction*. London: Sage.

Van Dijk, T. A. (2005) War Rhetoric of a Little Ally. *Journal of Language and Politics*. John Benjamins Publishing Company. 69.

Van Leeuwen, T. (2001) Semiotics and Iconography. In: Van Leeuwen, T. ,Jewitt, C. (eds), *Handbook of Visual Analysis*. London: Sage, 92—118.

Van Leeuwen, T. (2005a) *Introducing Social Semiotics*. London: Routledge.

Van Leeuwen, T. (2008) *Discourse and Practice: New Tools for Critical Discourse Analysis*. New York, NY: Oxford University Press.

Van Leeuwen, T. (2011) *The Language ofColour: An Introduction*. London: Routledge.

Voloshinov, Valentin N (1973) *Marxism and the Philosophy of Language* (trans. Ladislav Matejka & I. R. Titunik). New York: Seminar Press.

Winfried, Nöth (1995) *Handbook of Semiotics*. Bloomington: Indiana University Press.

Xin Bin. (2005) *Critical Linguistic Theory and Application*. Shanghai: Shanghai Foreign Language Education Press.

Appendices

Appendix A List of Titles and Premiere Time of the Campaign Advertising in 2008

Candidate	McCain-Palin	Barack Obama
1	"Freedom" (Oct. 31, 2008)	"Stronger and Safer" (Oct. 31, 2008)
2	"Obama Praising McCain" (Oct. 31, 2008)	"Rearview Mirror" (Oct. 31, 2008)
3	Charlie Crist ad (Oct. 30, 2008)	"Something" (Oct. 31, 2008)
4	"TV Special" (Oct. 29, 2008)	"His Choice" (Oct. 30, 2008)
5	"Tiny" (Oct. 28, 2008)	"Better Off" (approx. Oct. 27, 2008)
6	"Compare" (Oct. 28, 2008)	"Steel" (approx. Oct. 27, 2008)
7	"Ladies and Gentlemen" (Oct. 24, 2008)	"New Subject" (Oct. 27, 2008)
8	"Sweat Equity" (Oct. 22, 2008)	"Defining Moment" (2-min ad, Oct. 26, 2008)
9	"Fight" (Oct. 16, 2008)	"Try This" (Oct. 24, 2008)
10	"Unethical" (Oct. 14, 2008)	No title (seen Oct. 23, 2008)
11	"Ambition" (Oct. 10, 2008)	"Not Us" (Oct. 18, 2008)
12	"Folks" (Oct. 8, 2008)	"It Gets Worse" (Oct. 17, 2008)
13	"Hypo" (Oct. 7, 2008)	"90 Percent" (Oct. 16, 2008)
14	"Dangerous" (Oct. 6, 2008)	"Lose" (Oct. 10, 2008)
15	"Tax Cutter" (Oct. 3, 2008)	"Barney" (approx. Oct. 10, 2008)
16	"Week" (Oct. 1, 2008)	"Looking at Him" (approx. Oct. 10, 2008)
17	"Rein" (Sept. 30, 2008)	"Tested" (Oct. 9, 2008)

Appendices

Candidate	McCain-Palin	Barack Obama
18	"Promise" (Sept. 27, 2008)	"Unravel" (Oct. 9, 2008)
19	"Mum" (Sept. 23, 2008)	"Mills" (Oct. 8, 2008)
20	"Chicago Machine" (Sept. 22, 2008)	"Buster" (approx. Oct. 8, 2008)
21	"Overseas" (Sept. 19, 2008)	"Taketh" (Oct. 8, 2008)
22	"Jim Johnson" (Sept. 19, 2008)	"The Subject" (Oct. 7, 2008)
23	"Advice" (Sept. 18, 2008)	"This Year" (Oct. 6, 2008)
24	"Ohio Jobs" (Sept. 18, 2008)	"One Word" (Oct. 6, 2008)
25	"Michigan Jobs" (Sept. 18, 2008)	"Can't Explain" (Oct. 3, 2008)
26	"Dome" (Sept. 18, 2008)	"Spending Spree" (Oct. 1, 2008)
27	"Foundation" (Sept. 17, 2008)	"Two Extremes" (approx. Sept. 30, 2008)
28	"Enough is Enough" (Sept. 16, 2008)	"Same Path" (Sept. 30, 2008)
29	"Crisis" (Sept. 15, 2008)	"Figured" (Sept. 30, 2008)
30	"Disrespectful" (Sept. 12, 2008)	"Life Member" (Sept. 29, 2008)
31	"Fact Check" (Sept. 10, 2008)	"Parachute" (Sept. 29, 2008)
32	"Education" (Sept. 9, 2008)	"A Stronger Economy" (Sept. 25, 2008)
33	"Original Mavericks" (Sept. 8, 2008)	"Foreign Vehicles" (Sept. 23, 2008)
34		"Burden" (Sept. 16, 2008)
35		"Honor" (Sept. 15, 2008)
36		"His Administration" (Sept. 14, 2008)
37		"Real Change" (Sept. 12, 2008)
38		"Still" (Sept. 12, 2008)
39		"What Kind" (Sept. 9, 2008)
40		"No Maverick" (Sept. 8, 2008)
41		"Same" (Sept. 2, 2008)

Appendix B List of Titles and Premiere time of the campaign advertising in 2012

Candidates	Barak Obama	Romney
1	"Cynical" (Nov. 1, 2012).	"Iowa Newspapers Agree" (Nov. 1, 2012)
2	"Solid" (Nov. 1, 2012)	"Secretary of Business" (Nov. 1, 2012)
3	"Collapse" (Oct. 29, 2012).	No title (seen Oct. 31, 2012)
4	"Sleepless" (Oct. 28, 2012).	"Crushed by Your Policies" (Oct. 30, 2012)
5	"Remember" (Oct. 27, 2012)	"Who Will Do More?" (Oct. 27, 2012)
6	No title (seen Oct. 28, 2012)	Cabinet members ad (seen Oct. 26, 2012)
7	"Unbreakable" (Oct. 26, 2012)	"Highest Responsibility" (Oct. 23, 2012)
8	"No One Was Looking" (Oct. 25, 2012)	"The Clear Path" (Oct. 23, 2012)
9	"What He'll Do" (Oct. 25, 2012)	"Apology Tour" (Oct. 23, 2012)
10	"He's Got it Right" (Oct. 24, 2012)	"Find a Way" (Oct. 21, 2012)
11	"537" (Oct. 24, 2012)	"The Obama Plan" (Oct. 20, 2012)
12	"Determination" (Oct. 23, 2012)	"Bringing People Together" (Oct. 19, 2012)
13	"Rebuilding" (Oct. 22, 2012)	"Sarah" (Oct. 18, 2012)
14	"Commitment" (Oct. 20, 2012)	"The Choice" (Oct. 17, 2012)
15	"Made in Ohio" (Oct. 19, 2012)	"Fiscal Discipline" (Oct. 14, 2012)
16	"Wonderful" (Oct. 19, 2012)	"Helping the Middle Class" (Oct. 10, 2012)
17	"Seen" (Oct. 18, 2012)	"Putting Jobs First" (Oct. 10, 2012)
18	"Character" (Oct. 15, 2012)	"$5 Trillion" (Oct. 7, 2012)
19	"Main Street" (Oct. 15, 2012)	"Melanie" (Oct. 6, 2012)
20	"Challenges" (Oct. 13, 2012)	"Ohio Jobs" (Oct. 5, 2012)
21	"Decision" (Oct. 12, 2012)	"Born and Raised in Nevada" (Oct. 5, 2012)
22	"Economic Growth" (Oct. 12, 2012)	"Facts Are Clear" (Oct. 5, 2012)
23	"Strong Leader" (Oct. 11, 2012)	"Who Will Raise Taxes?" (Oct. 4, 2012)

Appendices

Candidates	Barak Obama	Romney
24	"Earned" (Oct. 9, 2012)	"12 Million Jobs" (Oct. 4, 2012)
25	"Only Choice" (Oct. 9, 2012)	"Many Americans" (Oct. 3, 2012)
26	"Policy" (Oct. 8, 2012)	"Already Has" (Oct. 2, 2012)
27	"Dishonest" (Oct. 6, 2012)	"Bankrupt" (Sept. 27, 2012)
28	"Trust" (Oct. 4, 2012)	"Too Many Americans" (Sept. 26, 2012)
29	"Mandatory" (Oct. 2, 2012)	"Stand Up to China" (Sept. 24, 2012)
30	"Since When" (Oct. 1, 2012)	"Mute Button" (Sept. 23, 2012)
31	"Care" (Sept. 29, 2012)	"Least We Can Do" (Sept. 20, 2012)
32	"My Job" (Sept. 27, 2012)	"War on Coal" (Sept. 19, 2012)
33	"Table" (Sept. 27, 2012)	"Way of Life" (Sept. 19, 2012)
34	"To Us" (Sept. 26, 2012)	"Dear Daughter" (Sept. 18, 2012)
35	"Fair Share" (Sept. 25, 2012)	"Failing American Families" (Sept. 17, 2012)
36	"No Taxes" (Sept. 24, 2012)	"The Romney Plan" (Sept. 17, 2012)
37	"Not One of Us" (Sept. 23, 2012)	"Failing American Workers" (Sept. 13, 2012)
38	"Preserving" (Sept. 20, 2012)	"A Better Future " (Sept. 9, 2012)
39	"Pay the Bills" (Sept. 18, 2012)	"A Better Future: Colorado - Defense"
40	"Tires" (Sept. 17, 2012)	"A Better Future: Florida - Defense"
41	"The Question" (Sept. 15, 2012)	"Give Me a Break" (Sept. 6, 2012).
42	"The Cheaters" (Sept. 14, 2012)	
43	"The Choice" updated (Sept. 12, 2012)	
44	"Guide" (Sept. 12, 2012)	
45	"Won't Say" (Sept. 12, 2012)	
46	"Dangerous" (Sept. 11, 2012)	
47	"Heavy Load" (Sept. 3, 2012)	

Appendix C List of Titles and Premiere Time of the Campaign Advertising in 2016

Candidates	Hillary Clinton	Donald J. Trump
1	"Tomorrow" (Nov. 7, 2016)	"Donald Trump's Argument For America" (Nov. 4, 2016)
2	"Roar" (Nov. 5, 2016)	"Unfit" (Nov. 3, 2016)
3	"We are America" (Nov. 3, 2016)	"United" (Nov. 2, 2016)
4	"Situation Room" (Nov. 2, 2016)	"Corruption" (Nov. 2, 2016)
5	"What He Believes" (Nov. 1, 2016)	"Choice" (Nov. 1, 2016)
6	"Daisy" (Oct. 31, 2016)	"Rebuilding the American Dream" (Oct. 20, 2016)
7	"On The Ballot" (Oct. 28, 2016)	"Predators" (Oct. 19, 2016)
8	"Bryce" (Oct. 27, 2016)	"Laura" (Oct. 19, 2016)
9	"Example" (Oct. 26, 2016)	"Change" (Oct 18, 2016)
10	"Families First" (Oct. 26, 2016)	"Deals" (Oct. 18, 2016)
11	"General Allen" (Oct. 25, 2016)	"Corruption" (Oct. 12, 2016)
12	"Barbershop" (Oct. 24, 2016)	"Dangerous" (Oct. 11, 2016)
13	"Captain Khan" (Oct. 21, 2016)	"Consumer Benefit" (Oct. 6, 2016)
14	"A Place for Everyone" (Oct. 19, 2016)	"Listening" (Oct. 4, 2016)
15	"Dallas Morning News" (Oct. 17, 2016)	"Motherhood" (Sept. 30, 2016)
16	"America's Bully" (Oct. 17, 2016)	"Why" (Sept. 30, 2016)
17	"Show Up" (Oct. 14, 2016)	"Movement" (Sept. 20, 2016)
18	"Measure" (Oct. 6, 2016)	"Deplorable" (Sept. 12, 2016)
19	"Arrogant" (Oct. 3, 2016)	
20	"Watch" (Sept. 27, 2016)	
21	"Investigation" (Sept. 25, 2016)	
22	"Mirrors" (Sept. 23, 2016)	
23	"Sees" (Sept. 21, 2016)	
24	"Low Opinion" (Sept. 13, 2016)	
25	"Agree" (Sept. 10, 2016)	
26	"Only Way" (Sept. 9, 2016)	
27	"Sacrifice" (Sept. 6, 2016)	

Appendix D Collections of Adopted Verbal and Visual Corpora: Positive Televised Campaign Advertising

Data 1

"Something": 30-second ad run in key states starting Oct. 31, 2008 (announced Oct. 30).

Male Announcer: Something's happening in America. In small towns and big cities, people from every walk of life unite in common purpose. A leader will bring us together.

Obama (clip from speech): We can choose hope over fear, and unity over division, the promise of change over the power of the status quo. That's how we'll emerge from this crisis stronger and more prosperous as one nation and as one people.

Obama (voiceover): I'm Barack Obama, and I approve this message.

Data 2

"Defining Moment": Two-minute ad run in key states starting Oct. 26, 2008 (announced Oct. 25).

"Defining Moment" 1

"Defining Moment" 2

"Defining Moment" 3

"Defining Moment" 3

"Defining Moment" 5

"Defining Moment" 6

"Defining Moment" 7

"Defining Moment" 8

"Defining Moment" 9

Obama: At this defining moment in our history, the question is not, "Are you better off than you were four years ago?" We all know the answer to that. The real question is "will our country be better off four years from now"? How will we lift our economy and restore America's place in the world? Here's what I'll do as President. To deal with our current emergency, I'll launch a rescue plan for the middle class. That begins with a tax cut for ninety-five percent of working Americans. If you have a job, pay taxes and make less than two hundred thousand dollars-a-year, you'll get a tax cut. I'll end the tax breaks for companies that ship our jobs overseas, and give them to companies that create jobs here in America. And I'll make low-cost loans available to small businesses. To build our economy for the future, I'll focus on our urgent national priorities: reducing the cost of health care, breaking our dependence on foreign oil and making sure that every child gets the education they need to compete. How will I pay for these priorities? First, we've got to stop spending ten billion dollars a month in Iraq, while they run up a surplus. I'll end this war responsibly, so we can invest here at home. We'll monitor the Wall Street rescue plan carefully, making sure taxpayers are protected and CEOs don't game the system. I'll let the temporary Bush tax cuts for the wealthiest 2% expire and close the corporate tax loopholes the lobbyists put in. I'll order a top-to-bottom audit of government spending and eliminate programs that don't work. We face real challenges. They won't be easy to solve. But we can do it if we end the mindless partisanship: the divisiveness, curb special interest power and restore our sense of common purpose. I'm Barack Obama. I approve this message and ask for your vote. Because if we stand together, we can meet our challenges and ensure that there are better days ahead.

Data 3

"Same Path" (Positive): 2-minute ad run in key states, announced Sept. 30, 2008.

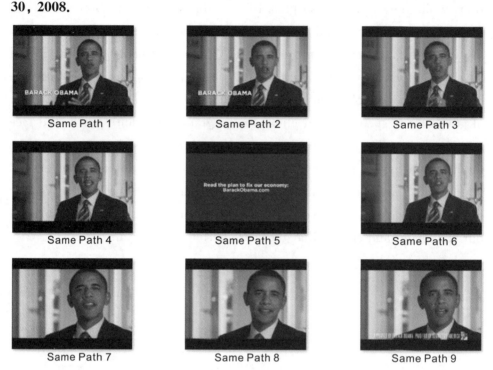

Obama: For eight years, we've been told that the way to a stronger economy was to give huge tax breaks to corporations and the wealthiest Americans and somehow prosperity would trickle down. Well now we know the truth. It didn't work. Instead of prosperity trickling down, pain has trickled up. Working family incomes have fallen by two thousand dollars a year. We're losing jobs. Deficits are exploding. Our economy is in turmoil. I know that we can steer ourselves out of this crisis. But not by driving down the very same path. And that's what this election's all about. On taxes, John McCain and I have very different ideas. Instead of giving hundreds of billions in new tax breaks to big corporations and oil companies, I'll cut taxes for small and startup businesses that are the backbone of our economy. Instead of more tax breaks for corporations that outsource American jobs, I'll give them to companies who create jobs here. Instead of extending the Bush tax cuts for the wealthiest, I'll focus on you. My plan offers three times as much tax relief to the middle class as Senator McCain's. If you make less than a quarter million a year, you won't see your taxes raised one penny under my plan. And seniors making less than fifty thousand, who are struggling with the rising costs of food and drugs on fixed incomes, won't pay income taxes at all. The tax code we have today is over 10,000 pages long. Almost every bit of it was shaped by some lobbyist taking care of some special interest. Well, it's time we had a President who puts you first. I hope you'll log on to Barack Obama. com and read my full plan. It will help jump-start our economy, create millions of jobs, and bring back our Main Streets all across America. The old trickle-down theory has failed us. We can't afford four more years like the last eight. I'm Barack Obama, and I approved this message. Because I know that with a new direction, and new policies focused on jobs and the middle class. We can lift our economy and our country.

Data 4

"Figured" (Positive): 30-second ad run in key states, from Sept. 30, 2008.

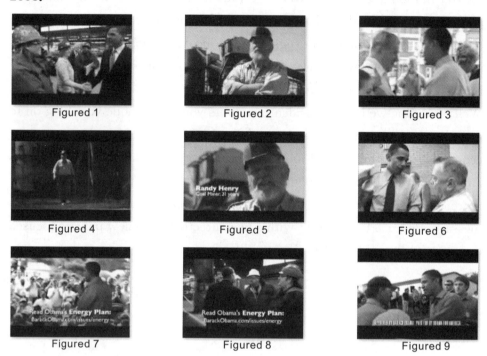

Obama: I'm Barack Obama, and I approve this message.

Randy Henry (coal miner, 31 years): Barack originates from Chicago, but he came to Southern Illinois and seen the devastation and the loss of the jobs in this coal industry. Washington, DC is not listening to us. Barack understands this.

Male Announcer: In Illinois and the US Senate, Barack Obama helped lead the fight for clean coal, to protect our environment and save good-paying American jobs.

Randy Henry: He's figured it out. It takes trust in each other to get the job done.

Data 5

"Freedom" (Positive): 30-second ad run in key states, announced Oct. 31, 2008.

McCain (voiceover): I've served my country since I was 17 years old. And, I spent five years longing for her shores. I came home dedicated to a cause greater than my own. We can grow our economy. We will cut government waste. Do hope for a stronger America. Vote for one. Join me.

Male Announcer: McCain.

McCain (voiceover): I'm John McCain. And I approve this message.

Data 6

Charlie Crist ad(Positive): 30-second ad run in FL, reported by Jonathan Martin, Politico, on Oct. 30, 2008.

Gov. Crist: Hi, I'm Charlie Crist. Our next president will face enormous challenges. For me, the choice is clear. John McCain is an American hero. He's a conservative, who knows to move America forward. We must work together. John McCain's uniquely qualified to lead our nation through a crisis. A reformer, a maverick, he'll fight out of control spending and keep our taxes down. John McCain never quits, and he'll always fight for you. Join me November 4th in voting for John McCain.

McCain: I'm John McCain and I approve this message.

Data 7

"Fight" (Positive): 60-second ad run nationally, announced Oct. 16, 2008.

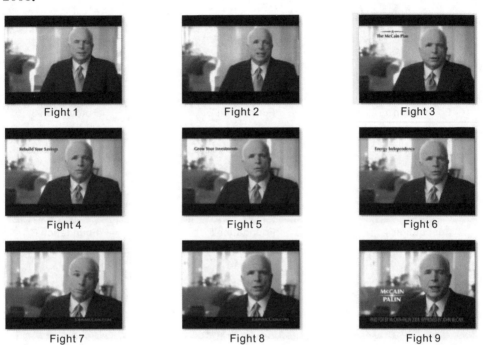

Fight 1　　　　　Fight 2　　　　　Fight 3
Fight 4　　　　　Fight 5　　　　　Fight 6
Fight 7　　　　　Fight 8　　　　　Fight 9

<u>McCain</u>: The last eight years haven't worked very well, have they? I'll make the next four better. Your savings, your job and your financial security are under siege. Washington is making it worse, bankrupting us with their spending. Telling us paying higher taxes is "patriotic"? And saying we need to "spread the wealth around"? They refuse common sense solutions for energy independence. Every day we send billions to the Middle East. We need a new direction, and I have a plan. Your savings. We'll rebuild them. Your investments. They'll grow again. Energy. We'll drill here and we'll create a renewable energy economy. Lower taxes and less spending will protect your job and create new ones. That'll restore our country. Stand up with me! Let's fight for America. I'm John McCain and I approve this message.

Data 8

"Foundation"(Positive): 30-second ad run nationally announced Sept. 17, 2008.

McCain: You, the American workers, are the best in the world. But your economic security has been put at risk by the greed of Wall Street. That's unacceptable. My opponent's only solutions are talk and taxes. I'll reform Wall Street and fix Washington. I've taken on tougher guys than this before.

Female Announcer: Change is coming. John McCain.

McCain: I'm John McCain and I approve this message.

Appendices

Data 9

"Solid": 30 ad from Nov. 1, 2012 run in CO, FL, IA, MN, NV, NH, NC, OH, VA and WI.

CBS News: Will you endorse President Obama?

Colin Powell: Yes. When he took over, we were in one of the worst recessions we had seen in recent times, close to the depression. And I saw, over the next several years, stabilization come back in the financial community. Housing is starting to pick up. The President saved the auto industry and the actions he has taken with respect to protect us from terrorism have been very solid. And so I think we ought to keep on the track that we are on.

Obama (voiceover): I'm Barack Obama and I approved this message.

Data 10

"Character": 30 ad from Oct. 15, 2012 run in OH.

John Glenn: Growing up in Ohio, you learn to size up a person by their character, and that's why I am supporting President Obama. He stood firm against the doubters and helped rescue the auto industry. He has taken on big corporations and foreign powers when they have threatened our jobs, our freedom, our way of life. And you know he means what he says. That is the Ohio way. Barack Obama has earned my vote, and my trust.

Obama (voiceover): I'm Barack Obama and I approve this message.

Appendices

Data 11

"Determination": 60 ad from Oct. 23, 2012 run in CO, FL, IA, NV, NH, NC, OH, VA and WI.

Determination 1 Determination 2 Determination 3

Determination 4 Determination 5 Determination 6

Determination 7 Determination 8 Determination 9

Obama (voiceover): There is just no quit in America and you are seeing that right now. Over five million new jobs. Exports up forty-one percent. Home values rising. Our auto industry back. And our heroes are coming home. We are not there yet but we've made real progress and the last thing we should do is to turn back now.

Obama (to camera): Here is my plan for the next four years: Making education and training a national priority; building on our manufacturing boom; boosting American-made energy; reducing the deficits responsibly by cutting where we can, and asking the wealthy to pay a little more and ending the war in Afghanistan so we can do some nation-building here at home. That's the right path. So read my plan. Compare it to Governor Romney's and Decide which is better for you. It is an honor to be your President, and I am asking for your vote so together. we can keep moving America forward.

Obama (voiceover): I am Barack Obama and I approved this message.

Data 12

"Iowa Newspapers Agree": 30 ad from Nov. 1, 2012.

Iowa Newspapers Agree 1   Iowa Newspapers Agree 1   Iowa Newspapers Agree 1

Iowa Newspapers Agree 1   Iowa Newspapers Agree 1   Iowa Newspapers Agree 1

Iowa Newspapers Agree 1   Iowa Newspapers Agree 1   Iowa Newspapers Agree 1

Male Announcer: "Mitt Romney offers a fresh economic vision." With those words, The Des Moines Register makes history, endorsing Mitt Romney for president. It is the paper's first endorsement of a Republican in forty years. Mitt Romney has earned the support of every major newspaper in Iowa. "A strong record of achievement in both the private and the public sectors." Voters should give Mitt Romney a chance to "correct the nation's fiscal course" and to "implode the partisan gridlock".

Romney (voiceover): I'm Mitt Romney and I approved this message.

Appendices | 195

Data 13

"The Clear Path": 60 ad from Oct. 23, 2012

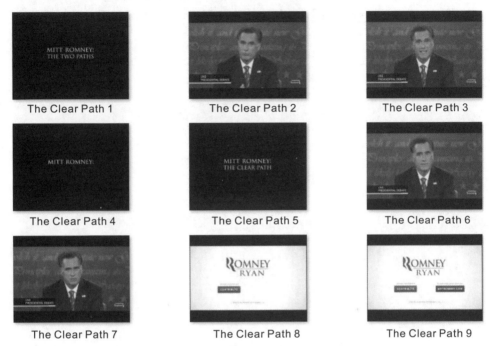

Mitt Romney: The Two Paths.

Romney (Oct. 22, 2012 debate): There are two very different paths the country can take. One is a path represented by the President, which, at the end of four years, would mean we would have $20 trillion in debt, heading towards Greece. I'll get us on track to a balanced budget. The President's path will mean continuing declining in take-home pay. I want to make sure our take-home pay turns around and starts to grow. The President's path means 20 million people out of work struggling for a good job. I'll get people back to work with 12 million new jobs. I'm going to make sure that we get people off of food stamps not by cutting the program but by getting them good jobs. America is going to come back. And for that to happen, we're going to have to have a president who can work across the aisle.

Mitt Romney: The Clear Path.

Romney (Oct. 22, 2012 debate): I'll work with you. I'll lead you in an open and honest way. And I ask for your vote. I'd like to be the next

President of the United States to support and help this great nation and to make sure that we all together maintain America as the hope of the earth.

Romney (voiceover): I am Mitt Romney, and I approved this message.

Data 14

"The Romney Plan": 30 ad from Sept. 17, 2012.

The Romney Plan 1 The Romney Plan 2 The Romney Plan 3
The Romney Plan 4 The Romney Plan 5 The Romney Plan 6
The Romney Plan 7 The Romney Plan 8 The Romney Plan 9

<u>Mitt Romney</u>: My plan is to help the middle class. Trade has to work for America. That means crack down on cheaters. It means open up new markets. Next, You have got to balance the budget. You have got to cut the deficit. You have got to stop spending more money than we take in. And finally, champion small business. Have tax policies, regulations, and healthcare policies that help small business. We put those in place. we will add 12 million new jobs in four years.

<u>Romney (voiceover)</u>: I am Mitt Romney and I approved this message.

Data 15

"Tomorrow": 2:00 ad run nationally on Election Eve Nov. 7, 2016.

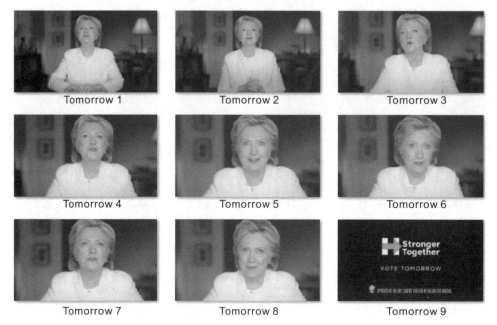

Clinton (to camera): I think we can all agree it has been a long campaign. But tomorrow, you get to pick our next president. So here are a few things that I hope you'll think about. First, it is not just my name and my opponent's name on the ballot. It is the kind of country we want for our children and grandchildren. Is America dark and divisive or hopeful and inclusive? Our core values are being tested in this election. But everywhere I go people are refusing to be defined by fear and division. Look! we, we all know we've come through some hard economic times and we've some pretty big changes. But I believe in our people. I love this country, and I am convinced our best days are still ahead of us if we reach for them together. I want to be a president for all Americans, not just those who support me in this election, but for everyone. Because we all have a role to play in building a stronger, fairer America. The second thing I want you to know is this. I will work my heart out as president to make life better for you and your family. We won't always get it right, but you can count on this. I've never quit, and I never will. I'll get up every day determined to keep America safe and strong and make our economy work for everyone, not just those at the top. And finally, working for children and families has been the cause of my life, but it has never been more important than it is right now. This has to be our mission together, to give our kids and every American the chance to live up to their God-given potential. So tonight I'm asking for your vote, and tomorrow let's make history together. I am Hillary Clinton, and one last time I approve this message. I am Hillary Clinton and I approve this message.

Data 16

"Families First": 0:30 ad run in FL, IA, NV, NH, NC, OH, PA and on national cable from Oct. 26, 2016.

Hillary Clinton: Too many families today don't earn what they need and they don't have the opportunities they deserve. I believe families deserve quality education for their kids, child care they can trust and afford, equal pay for women, and jobs they can really live on. People ask me, what will be different if I am president? Well, kids and families have been the passion of my life, and they will be the heart of my presidency.

Clinton (voiceover): I am Hillary Clinton and I approve this message.

Appendices

Data 17

"A Place for Everyone" 0:60 ad run in FL, IA, NV, NH, NC, OH and PA from Oct. 19, 2016.

A Place for Everyone 1
A Place for Everyone 2
A Place for Everyone 3
A Place for Everyone 4
A Place for Everyone 5
A Place for Everyone 6
A Place for Everyone 7
A Place for Everyone 8
A Place for Everyone 9

Clinton: This is not an ordinary time and this is not an ordinary election. I want to send a message to every boy and girl and indeed to the entire world that America already is great, but we are great because we are good. We are going to life each other up. I want us to heal our country and bring it together. We have to start getting the economy to work for everyone, not just those at the top; making the best education system from pre-school through college, making it affordable, because that is I think the best way to get the future that our children and grandchildren deserve. My vision of America is an America where everyone has a place. This is the America that I know and love. If we set those goals and we go together, there's nothing that America can't do.

Clinton (voiceover): I am Hillary Clinton and I approve this message.

Data 18

"Measure": 0:60 ad run in FL, IA, NV, NC, OH and PA and on cable from Oct. 6, 2016.

Woman's voice (from home video): How tall are you?

Hillary Clinton (voiceover): How do we measure greatness in America? The height of our skyscrapers? The size of our bank accounts? No. It's measured by what we do for our children. The values we pass on.

[to camera]: I have spent my life fighting for kids and families and it will be my mission to build a country where our children can rise as high as their dreams and hard work take them. That means good schools for every child in every zip code, college that leads to opportunities, not debt, and an economy where every young American can find a job that let them start a family of their own. We face big challenges but we can solve them the same way families do. Work together! one another, and never giving up. I want our success to be measured by theirs. I am Hillary Clinton and I approve this message.

Appendices

Data 19

"United": 0:30 ad run in major markets from Nov. 2, 2016.

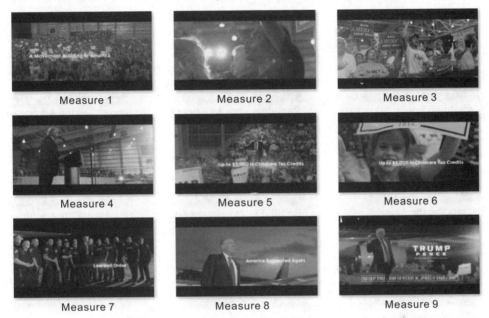

Measure 1   Measure 2   Measure 3
Measure 4   Measure 5   Measure 6
Measure 7   Measure 8   Measure 9

<u>Male Announcer</u>: There is a movement building in America. Everyday people stand united Be ready to replace decades of broken politics with a new leader who's not a part of the system. Donald Trump. His plan: Lower taxes. Families get childcare tax credits. Law and Order is balanced with justice and fairness, and America is respected in the world again. This is our country. We can change directions and make America great again.

<u>Trump (voiceover)</u>: I am Donald Trump, and I approve this message.

Data 20

"Rebuilding the American Dream": 0:30 ad run in battleground states from Oct. 20, 2016.

Rebuilding the American dream 1

Rebuilding the American dream 2

Rebuilding the American dream 3

Rebuilding the American dream 4

Rebuilding the American dream 5

Rebuilding the American dream 6

Rebuilding the American dream 7

Rebuilding the American dream 8

Rebuilding the American dream 9

<u>Male Announcer</u>: It takes a builder to rebuild the American Dream, and Donald Trump has the blueprint. Tax relief for working people. A 30-percent tax cut. Peace of mind for working families. An average $5,000 childcare tax reduction. And paid maternity leave. Lower healthcare costs. Expanding competition by allowing people to purchase coverage across state lines. This is the blueprint. This is the builder. Donald Trump.

<u>Trump (voiceover)</u>: I am Donald Trump, and I approve this message.

Data 21

"Listening": 0:30 ad run nationally and in battleground states from Oct. 4, 2016.

(Monica C., Philadelphia, PA)

I love being a mom. But no matter how hard we work, we can't get ahead. Childcare costs have us stuck. Donald Trump is listening.

Trump (clip from speech): My childcare plan allows for every family in America to deduct their childcare expenses from their income taxes.

Monica C: His childcare plan makes a difference for working families. More money, more freedom. He's helping Americans just like us.

Trump: I am Donald Trump, and I approve this message.

Negative Televised Campaign Advertising
Data 22
"His Choice": 30-second ad run in key states starting Oct. 30, 2008.

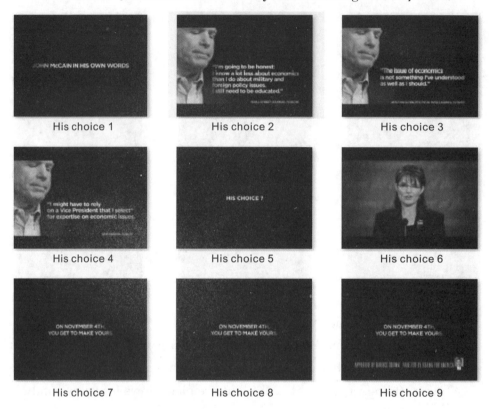

Text on screen:

<u>John McCain in his own words</u>: I am going to be honest. I know a lot less about economics that I do about military and foreign policy issues. I still need to be educated. The issue of economics is not something I've understood as well as I should. I might have to rely on a Vice President that I select for expertise on economic issues.

<u>Male Announcer</u>: His choice? On November 4th, You Get to Make Yours

<u>Obama (voiceover)</u>: I am Barack Obama, and I approve this message.

Data 23

"Unravel": 30-second ad run in key states from approx. Oct. 9, 2008.

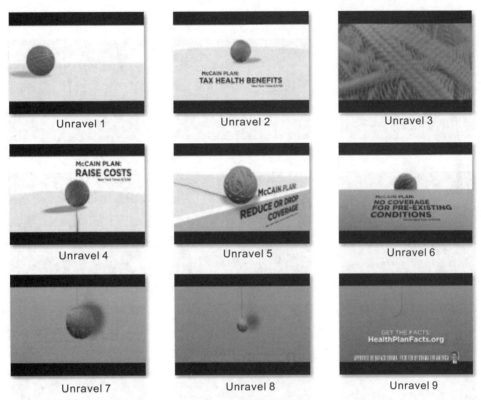

Obama: I am Barack Obama and I approve this message.

Male Announcer: It could all unravel. Your health care under John McCain. McCain would tax health benefits for the first time ever, meaning higher income taxes for millions. His plan would raise costs for employers offering health care, so your coverage would be reduced or even dropped completely. And since McCain won't require coverage for pre-existing conditions, finding a new plan could leave you hanging by a thread. It is not the change we need.

Data 24

"One Word": 30-second ad run in key states, starting Oct. 6, 2008 (announced Oct. 4).

Obama: I am Barack Obama, and I approve this message.

Male Announcer: On health care, John McCain promises a tax credit. But here is what he won't tell you: McCain would impose a new tax on health benefits, taxing your health care for the first time ever. It is a multi-trillion dollar tax hike, the largest middle-class tax increase in history. You won't find one word about it on his website. But the McCain tax could cost your family thousands. Can you afford it?

Appendices

Data 25

"Tiny": 30-second ad run in key Florida markets, announced Oct. 28, 2008.

Male Announcer: Iran. Radical Islamic government. Known sponsors of terrorism. Developing nuclear capabilities to generate power, but threatening to eliminate Israel. Obama says Iran is a "tiny" country, "doesn't pose a serious threat." Terrorism, destroying Israel, those aren't "serious threats?" Obama is dangerously unprepared to be President.

McCain: I'm John McCain and I approve this message.

Data 26

"Ladies and Gentlemen": 30-second ad run in key states, announced Oct. 24, 2008.

Ladies and Gentlemen 1

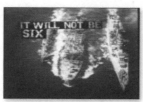
Ladies and Gentlemen 2

Ladies and Gentlemen 3

Ladies and Gentlemen 4

Ladies and Gentlemen 5

Ladies and Gentlemen 6

Ladies and Gentlemen 7

Ladies and Gentlemen 8

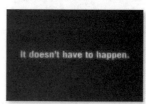
Ladies and Gentlemen 9

Male Announcer: Listen to Joe Biden. Talking about what electing Barack Obama will mean.

Biden (audio): Mark my words. It will not be six months before the world tests Barack Obama. The world is looking. We're going to have an international crisis to test the mettle of this guy. I guarantee you it's gonna happen.

Announcer: It doesn't have to happen. Vote McCain.

McCain (voiceover): I'm John McCain and I approve this message.

Data 27

"Education": 30-second ad run in key states announced Sept. 9, 2008.

Male Announcer: *Education Week* says Obama "hasn't made a significant mark on education." That he is "elusive" on accountability. A "staunch defender of the existing public school monopoly". Obama's one accomplishment. Legislation to teach "comprehensive sex education" to kindergartners. Learning about sex before learning to read. Barack Obama. Wrong on education. Wrong for your family.

McCain: I am John McCain and I approved this message.

Data 28

"Decision":30 ad from Oct. 12, 2012 run in CO, FL, IA, NV, OH and VA.

Female Announcer: As you're making your decision, maybe you're wondering what to believe about Mitt Romney. Well when it comes to protect your access to birth control and the basic women's health care services, Planned Parenthood provides one thing we must remember is this:

Romney (clip): I'll cut off funding to Planned Parenthood.

Female Announcer: He'll cut it off. Cut us off.

Romney (clip): Planned Parenthood, we're going to get rid of that.

Female Announcer: Women need to know the real Mitt Romney.

Obama (voiceover): I'm Barack Obama and I approved this message.

Appendices

Data 29

"My Job" :30 ad from Sept. 27, 2012.

Obama: I am Barack Obama and I approve this message.

Romney: There are 47 percent of the people who will vote for the president no matter what ... who are dependent upon government, who believe that they are victims, who believe the government has a responsibility to care for them, who believe that they are entitled to health care, to food, to housing, to you-name-it. And they will vote for this president no matter what. And so my job is not to worry about those people. I'll never convince them that they should take personal responsibility and care for their lives.

Data 30

"To Us": 30 ad from Sept. 26, 2012.

Obama: I am Barack Obama and I approve this message.

Male Announcer: When Mitt Romney left Bain, hundreds of plants, factories, and stores were shuttered. Workers saw their wages slashed, their jobs sent overseas. Romney made a fortune. Now he wants to bring that business experience to us. He would keep tax breaks for outsourcing and hand new tax cuts to millionaires all while raising taxes on the middle class. Romney is not the solution. He is the problem.

Data 31

"won't Say": 30 ad announced Sept. 12, 2012 run in IA, NV, OH and VA.

Obama (voiceover): I am Barack Obama and I approve this message.

Male Announcer: Mitt Romney. He won't reveal what is in his taxes. And he won't tell you what he would do to YOURS. To pay for huge new tax breaks for millionaires like him, Romney would have to raise taxes on the middle class. "Two thousand dollars for a family with children", says a non-partisan report. You could lose the deduction for your home mortgage, college tuition and health care. How much would you pay? Romney just won't say.

Data 32

"The Obama Plan": 30 ad from Oct. 20, 2012.

The Obama Plan 1

The Obama Plan 2

The Obama Plan 3

The Obama Plan 4

The Obama Plan 5

The Obama Plan 6

The Obama Plan 7

The Obama Plan 8

The Obama Plan 9

<u>Male Announcer</u>: If Barack Obama is reelected, what will the next four years be like? One. The debt will grow from $16 trillion to $20 trillion. Two. Twenty million Americans could lose their employer-based health care. Three. Taxes on the middle class will go up by $4,000. Four. Energy prices will continue to go up. And five. $716 billion in Medicare cuts that hurt current seniors. Five reasons we can't afford four more years of Barack Obama.

<u>Romney (voiceover)</u>: I am Mitt Romney, and I approved this message.

Data 33

"Way of Life": 30 ad from Sept. 19, 2012

Man: My family has worked in the coal industry for over sixty years; this is the way of life we know. The policies that the current administration has got is attacking my livelihood. Obama said he was going to bankrupt any new power plants that opened up that's coal-fired and he's keeping his promise. I got two young grandsons. I'm scared for their future, let alone mine. I support Mitt Romney.

Romney (voiceover): I am Mitt Romney and I approve this message.

Data 34

"Failing American Workers":30 ad from Sept. 13, 2012.

Failing American Workers 1

Failing American Workers 2

Failing American Workers 3

Failing American Workers 4

Failing American Workers 5

Failing American Workers 6

Failing American Workers 7

Failing American Workers 8

Failing American Workers 9

Male Announcer: This is America's manufacturing when President Obama took office. Under Obama, we've lost over half a million manufacturing jobs. Seven times Obama could have stopped cheating. Seven times he refused.

Romney: It's time to stand up to the cheaters and make sure we protect jobs for the American people.

Male Announcer: Barack Obama. Fail to stop cheating. Fail American workers.

Romney (voiceover): I am Mitt Romney and I approved this message.

Data 35

"Give Me a Break":30 ad from Sept. 6, 2012.

Give Me A Break 1 Give Me A Break 2 Give Me A Break 3
Give Me A Break 4 Give Me A Break 5 Give Me A Break 6
Give Me A Break 7 Give Me A Break 8 Give Me A Break 9

<u>Male Announcer</u>: As the economy gets worse, Barack Obama calls on Bill Clinton to help his failing campaign.

<u>Bill Clinton (in Obama ad "Clear Choice")</u>: It is about which candidate is more likely to return us to full employment.

<u>Male Announcer</u>: He is a good soldier, helping his party's president. But what did Bill Clinton say about Barack Obama in 2008?

<u>Bill Clinton (in Hanover, NH, Jan. 7, 2008)</u>: Give me a break. This whole thing is the biggest fairy tale I've ever seen.

<u>Male Announcer</u>: 23 million Americans struggling for work. A middle class falling further behind.

<u>Bill Clinton (in Hanover, NH, Jan. 7, 2008)</u>: Give me a break.

<u>Romney (voiceover)</u>: I'm Mitt Romney and I approved this message.

Data 36

"We Are America" 0:60 ad from Nov. 3, 2016, no info. on buy.

Clinton (voiceover): I am Hillary Clinton and I approve this message.

TEXT: We are America.

Trump (audio clips): I'd look her right in that fat ugly face of hers. He's a war hero' cause he was captured; I like people that weren't captured, okay? You got to see this guy. Oh, I don't know what I said. Ah, I don't remember. A person who's flat-chested is very hard to be a 10. Our military is a disaster. When Mexico sends its people, they're bringing drugs. They're rapists. I'd like to punch him in the face, I'll tell you. Get him out of here. Putting a wife to work is a very dangerous thing. Wouldn't you rather in a certain sense have Japan have nuclear weapons?

Announcer: Saudi Arabia.

Trump: Than Saudi Arabia, absolutely.

Chris Matthews: Talk of maybe using nuclear weapons. Nobody wants to hear that about an American president.

Trump: Then why are we making them? Why do we make them? I would bomb the [beep] out of them. I love war in a certain way.

TEXT: We are not him.

Data 37

"What He Believes" :0:60 ad run in AZ, FL, IA, NV, NC, OH and PA and on cable rom Nov. 1, 2016.

What He Believes 1 What He Believes 2 What He Believes 3
What He Believes 4 What He Believes 5 What He Believes 6
What He Believes 7 What He Believes 8 What He Believes 9

TEXT: He really believes this:

Trump: Putting a wife to work is a very dangerous thing.

TEXT: And this:

Trump: When I come home and dinner's not ready, I go through the roof.

TEXT: He really said this:

Trump: Grab 'em by the [beep] … and when you're a star they let you do it. You can do anything.

TEXT: And did this:

Lester Holt: More accusers coming forward to say they were sexually assaulted by Donald Trump.

Trump: And I'll go back stage before a show, and everyone's getting dressed.

News announcer: Donald Trump walked into the dressing room while contestants, some as young as 15 were changing.

Trump: They were standing there with no clothes. You see these incredible looking women.

TEXT: This is Donald Trump.

Trump: I'd look her right in that fat ugly face of hers.

Trump: She ate like a pig.

Trump: A person who's flat chested is very hard to be a 10.

Interviewer: Do you treat women with respect?

Trump: I can't say that either.

Interviewer: Alright, good.

TEXT: Anyone who believes, says, "does what he does?" "Is unfit to be president?"

Clinton (voiceover): I am Hillary Clinton and I approve this message.

Appendices

Data 38

"Low Opinion" :0:60 ad run on national cable from Sept. 13, 2016.

Low Opinion 1 Low Opinion 2 Low Opinion 3
Low Opinion 4 Low Opinion 5 Low Opinion 6
Low Opinion 7 Low Opinion 8 Low Opinion 9

Clinton (voiceover): I am Hillary Clinton and I approve this message.

Trump (clip): You can't lead this nation if you have such a low opinion for its citizens.

TEXT: What is Donald's opinion of our citizens?

Trump: How stupid are the people of the country?

Trump: We're buiding a wall. He is a Mexican.

Trump: Oh, I don't know what I said,ah; I don't remember.

Trump: You're living in poverty. Your schools are no good. You have no jobs. What the hell do you have to lose?

Trump: If you look at his wife, she had nothing to say. She probably maybe she wasn't allowed to have anything to say.

Trump: He is a war hero because he was captured. I like people that weren't captured. Okay, I hate to tell you.

Megyn Kelly: You've called women you don't like fat pigs, dogs, slobs and disgusting animals.

Trump: She is a disgusting pig, right?

Trump：I'd like to punch him in the face.

Trump：They are losers…losers…losers…disgusting…stupid.

Trump(clip)：You can't lead this nation if you have such a low opinion for its citizens.

TEXT：Exactly.

Data 39

"Unfit" ;0;30 ad run in major markets from Nov. 3, 2016.

Male Announcer: Decades of lies, cover-ups and scandal have finally caught up with Hillary Clinton. Hillary Clinton is under FBI investigation again after her emails were found on pervert Anthony Weiner's laptop. Think about that. America's most sensitive secrets (were) unlawfully sent, received and exposed by Hillary Clinton, her staff, and Anthony Weiner. Hillary cannot lead a nation while crippled by a criminal investigation.

Hillary Clinton: Unfit to serve.

Trump (voiceover): I am Donald Trump, and I approve this message.

Data 40

"Corruption": 0:30 ad run in major markets from Nov. 2, 2016.

Female Announcer: From dead broke to worth hundreds of millions. So how did Hillary end up filthy rich? Pay to play politics. Staggering amounts of cash poured into the Clinton Foundation from criminals, dictators, countries that hate America. Hillary cut deals for donors. Now the FBI has launched a new investigation. After decades of lies and scandal, her corruption is closing in.

Trump (voiceover): I am Donald Trump, and I approve this message.

Data 41

"Laura": 0:30 ad run in FL, IA, ME, PA and WI from Oct. 19, 2016.

<u>Trump (voiceover)</u>: I am Donald Trump, and I approve this message.

<u>Laura Wilkerson</u>: The man who murdered Joshua is an illegal alien. And he should not have been here.

The killer hit him on the head with a closet rod so hard that it broke in four pieces. And then he took him to a field and he doused him with gasoline and set him on fire. It was the hardest day of my life. Hillary Clinton's border policy is going to allow people into the country just like the one that murdered my son.

Data 42

"Dangerous": 0:30 ad run nationally and in battleground states from Oct. 11, 2016.

Male Announcer: Our next president faces daunting challenges in a dangerous world. Iran promoting terrorism, North Korea threatening, ISIS on the rise, Libya and North Africa in chaos. Hillary Clinton failed every single time as Secretary of State. Now she wants to be President. Hillary Clinton doesn't have the fortitude, strength or stamina to lead in our world. She failed as Secretary of State. Don't let her fail us again.

Trump (voiceover): I am Donald Trump, and I approve this message.